THE RELEVANT CLASSROOM

THE RELEVANT CLASSROOM

6 Steps to Foster Real-World Learning

ASCD
Alexandria, Virginia USA

Eric Hardie

1703 N. Beauregard St. • Alexandria, VA 22311-1714 USA
Phone: 800-933-2723 or 703-578-9600 • Fax: 703-575-5400
Website: www.ascd.org • E-mail: member@ascd.org
Author guidelines: www.ascd.org/write

Ronn Nozoe, *Interim CEO and Executive Director;* Stefani Roth, *Publisher;* Genny Ostertag, *Director, Content Acquisitions;* Susan Hills, *Senior Acquisitions Editor;* Julie Houtz, *Director, Book Editing & Production;* Liz Wegner, *Editor;* Judi Connelly, *Senior Art Director;* Masie Chong, *Graphic Designer;* Mary Duran, *Graphic Designer;* Keith Demmons, *Senior Production Designer;* Kelly Marshall, *Interim Manager, Production Services;* Trinay Blake, *E-Publishing Specialist*

All web links in this book are correct as of the publication date below but may have become inactive or otherwise modified since that time. If you notice a deactivated or changed link, please e-mail books@ascd.org with the words "Link Update" in the subject line. In your message, please specify the web link, the book title, and the page number on which the link appears.

PAPERBACK ISBN: 978-1-4166-2767-8   ASCD product #120003   n8/19
PDF E-BOOK ISBN: 978-1-4166-2769-2; see Books in Print for other formats.
Quantity discounts are available: e-mail programteam@ascd.org or call 800-933-2723, ext. 5773, or 703-575-5773. For desk copies, go to www.ascd.org/deskcopy.

Library of Congress Cataloging-in-Publication Data
Library of Congress Control Number:2019943017

29 28 27 26 25 24 23 22 21 20   1 2 3 4 5 6 7 8 9 10 11 12

To Krista, Alexa, Rachel, and Bryn,
for walking softly in the morning

THE RELEVANT CLASSROOM

Introduction

A recent conversation with a colleague reminded me why I wrote this book. We were talking about the school experiences of our own kids, when the conversation turned to her 13-year-old son. "He absolutely hates school," she lamented, "and I mean *hate*. Every morning is a huge fight. He finds the days long and says he's bored out of his mind. He's a smart enough kid and has interests outside of school—but sitting passively for hours of the day has killed any interest he had in school."

As a high school principal, I saw this issue manifest itself in the uptick in office referrals for behavior in the afternoon. A typical scenario goes something like this: Teacher calls the office to send a student down for misbehaving; the student slumps in an office chair; when asked what happened the student says, "Yes, I did that, but you have no idea how bored I was! Getting sent to the office is better than spending another minute there. You have no idea how long the days are here!"; teacher comes down at the end of the day to express her own frustration and is unsure how to improve the situation with the student despite her best efforts.

The unfortunate reality is that many students report finding school boring. It's one of the common threads between both those who perform well academically and those who don't. I have had many conversations with students who get good grades but say something like, "School's pretty boring, but I have my heart set on getting into a program, so I just keep at it."

1

This creates problems on multiple levels, for both students and teachers, and is one of the main reasons I wrote this book. The way that we do school—the structure, process, and expectations—means that school often does not work well for both students and teachers. There are myriad reasons why this is the case, and we will explore several of them in the chapters that follow, but suffice it to say the current system of teaching and learning is not working. Students are frequently disengaged, are not learning as much as they could, and too frequently drop out. Teachers are working too hard and are professionally frustrated, and too frequently *they* drop out as well, either literally or emotionally. It doesn't have to be this way.

About This Book

This book doesn't provide all the answers, but it does provide strategies that will help move us in the right direction by bridging the gap between the artificiality of the world of school and the real world that surrounds it. This is a major cause of disengagement: Students don't see the connection between what they are being asked to learn and do in school and the world around them. The strategies are purposefully broad so that, whether you teach kindergarten or grade 12, you will find them useful. While subjects and students change with age, the fundamentals remain the same. Really deep learning requires that certain criteria be met for magic to take place in the classroom.

First, students are engaged through meaningful work. "Why are we doing this?" is a time-honored and entirely legitimate question. When our answer is "Because it's in the curriculum," we are in trouble right out of the gate. By making meaning central to student work, we can provide real answers to this most important of questions; in fact, if done right, students won't even feel the need to ask it. Chapter 2 provides a number of strategies, guiding questions, and examples we can use to ensure that students are engaged in work that they see as purposeful.

One of the most common questions from teachers is "How do I do interesting things in my classroom and still cover the curriculum?" It's an important question, and part of the answer lies in putting the curriculum into context. If we start with the curriculum as a checklist of things that need to be covered, then, again, we are in trouble right out of the gate. If, however, we treat it as a list of skills and knowledge that students can use to support the meaningful work they are doing, then suddenly it makes more sense to students and they will understand why they are learning it. Chapter 3 unpacks how to do this successfully and provides some examples.

In Chapter 4, we'll explore the need to create space for students to learn. One common cause of disengagement in a traditional classroom is that there isn't space for the students and their interests, ideas, creativity, and skills. When a classroom is too focused on the teacher, it doesn't respect the individuality of the students and forces the teacher to work even harder. In this chapter, we'll talk about how to frame real-world challenges for students while leaving space for them to find themselves in the work.

Another important way to build engagement and relevance is to actively connect student work to the real world (we'll know our work to improve education is done when we don't have to use this designation anymore). School is a lot different for students when their actions and learning are being purposed to positively affect the world around them than when they are being used to complete a test. In Chapter 5, we'll talk about the importance of community connections and audience to communicate to students the value of the work they are engaged in.

With the groundwork laid, we can allow students to lead in our classrooms. By creating meaningful work and building leadership capacity in students, teachers can achieve that enviable goal of moving from being the sage on the stage to the guide on the side, while simultaneously expanding student learning. If we want students to become leaders, then they need to learn to lead in our classrooms. Leadership takes practice and requires opportunity and feedback to flourish. Chapter 6 talks about how we can best do this.

Finally, we can see deep learning and great success when providing feedback on and evaluating student work that is purposeful and meaningful. Making one of the more challenging parts of the job more enjoyable, while also deepening student understanding, is the subject of Chapter 7.

In the end, this is not about teaching—it's about *learning*. We can't learn for students, but we can create experiences where deep learning will take place. This is also not about teachers burning themselves out trying to make magic in the classroom every day. This is about recognizing that students are our greatest untapped source of creativity, collaboration, and innovation, and that tapping into these resources is the key to a new kind of classroom and deeper learning.

The Case for Change

At an education conference I recently attended that attracted educators from across North America and around the world, there were many ideas presented and debated about how to best improve education. There was one belief that seemed universal to all the participants: School needs to change. Suddenly, educators are being told to prepare students for jobs that "don't yet exist" in a world of exponential change. How are you supposed to prepare students for a life that has so much uncertainty? Our traditional paradigm of education was not made for this.

Harvard professor Tony Wagner provocatively describes the problem in his insightful book *The Global Achievement Gap*:

> In today's highly competitive global "knowledge economy," *all students need new skills* for college, careers, and citizenship. The failure to give all students these new skills leaves today's youth—and our country—at an alarming competitive disadvantage. Schools haven't changed; the world has. And so our schools are not failing. Rather, they are obsolete—even the ones that score the best on standardized tests. This is a very different problem requiring an altogether different solution. (2008, p. xxi)

So why do we persist in maintaining an increasingly obsolete system? The first step to finding that answer requires that we dig deeper into the nature of this obsolescence so that we can move toward a remedy. There is a nearly endless list of reasons for realigning schools around a deeper learning agenda, but here are some of the most pressing.

Current research from Gallup of nearly a million U.S. students indicates that while, on average, students in elementary school are generally interested in school, starting in grade 5, this number drops every year until grade 11, where it bottoms out at 44 percent before rebounding slightly (Brenneman, 2016). Unfortunately, numbers from Canada look equally glum. These statistics should serve as a wake-up call to educators in many parts of North America. It's clear from this survey that we face a crisis of disinterest, which is antithetical to our desire to leave students with a lifelong, abiding passion for learning. In practical terms, these numbers raise important questions about what students should be learning, how they can be engaged in their learning, and what input they should have into their learning and schools in order to turn this alarming trend around.

The World Has Changed Fundamentally. Has School?

It's hard to overstate the importance of the dramatic changes that have taken place in the world in the last 30 years that should have radically changed what takes place in the classroom. However, education has been slow to move (for reasons that we will discuss later), and the fundamental process and organization have changed very little since formal schooling's inception. The net result is that our students are not being adequately prepared for life after school today and are even less prepared for what life will look like in the future.

One thing that is striking about looking at photographs of classrooms of the past is that they, by and large, look the same as classrooms today. Yes, there may be some differences in fashion or the technology being used, but the stereotype of the teacher standing at the front of the classroom often holds today. A time traveler would still be able to identify a classroom.

School is based on an industry-inspired production line system where children enter at the age of 4 and emerge finished at the age of 18. In between, they learn to follow directions from their supervisor and sit quietly for hours on end doing what they are told, even when it's not particularly interesting to them, developing strategies to make the time go by. In other words, they are well suited to a production-line job. This, of course, is not an accident. The education system was designed by industrialists with these explicit goals in mind.

Curiously, if you look at historical versus modern photographs of other workplaces, they look very different. Picture a photo of workers in a woolen mill juxtaposed with workers at a social media or biotech company. The same time traveler would be less likely to process what was going on. How can the process for educating the citizens of the future be so firmly rooted in the past?

The Sources of Misalignment

How exactly is education so misaligned? Why is it no longer pointing students in the direction they need to go? Here are a few elements of the system that need rethinking.

The economics of grading. The use of grades as a classroom currency is a problem because (1) it's artificial and (2) it tends to prioritize skills that are unique to the classroom. It is difficult to find parallels between grades and the world outside education. In the workplace, we are more likely to have a performance review with some commendations and next steps for improvement, not a graded percentage. Because grades are largely a matter of judgment, they are not necessarily equal from one class to the next and thus difficult to discriminate between.

Getting good grades can be as much about attendance, short-term memory, compliance, and understanding what some students see as the game of education as it is about actual learning. How many times have you heard an underperforming student comment, "A 62 percent is good enough. As long as I'm passing"? It's far too common and always frustrating for educators. It makes clear two things about the student's thinking: (1) they've learned that school is about grades and not learning, and (2) they don't see grades as motivating, so there's not much reason to try. It's very difficult to get buy-in from students who have simply opted out of the system.

Daniel Pink (2009) argues in his book *Drive* that beyond basic biology, we are driven by the need for three things: autonomy, mastery, and purpose. Because many school systems put grades and learning on the same plane, and because it is much more driven by the adults than the students, it can be challenging to keep students motivated if they decide that they don't care how they do because autonomy, mastery, and purpose are in short supply. When their recognition of the artificiality of the school system is combined with a lack of intrinsic motivation and frustration over school's seeming irrelevance, the result is too often a dispiriting formula for dropping out.

Education versus certification. If the classroom economic system is based on grades, then the school economic system (at the high school level) is based on credit acquisition and diplomas. The standardization of courses means that students are expected to get a similarly well-rounded educational experience (particularly for the first couple of years of high school). However, it sometimes means that students drop out before they get to courses that might be of interest to them.

As a high school principal, I have clear recollections of trying to get a student named Alex through the system. Alex showed up to school every day looking ready for a day in construction, complete with steel-toed work boots and plaid jacket. He didn't like school very much because it wasn't relevant to him, and coaxing him through mandatory courses in science and math was a trial for all of us: Alex, his teachers, his parents, and the administration. It also meant that he would frequently get kicked out of class. However, if you invited Alex to help with side projects, like doing some landscaping at the front of the school, he worked harder than anyone and would never complain. We all knew that Alex would be happy once he reached the older grades and could do work placements and take classes in wood working and metal work, but getting him there was going to be a struggle. Despite our best efforts, he eventually dropped out of school a few credits short of graduation and is happily working construction, but it has always seemed unfortunate to me that we don't have a system that's flexible enough to support the countless students like Alex.

One of the gravest dangers to the current school system is the gap between education and certification. Schools rely on the educational economic system to extrinsically motivate students by granting high school diplomas that demonstrate the school's value. However, thanks to the proliferation of online schools, it has become easier and more flexible than ever to earn high school credits. In fact, we are entering a time when you could earn a high school diploma, earn an undergraduate degree, and do graduate work without ever entering a building. While this is terrific news for the educational consumer, it should also be providing a wake-up call to all school educators. If what you are offering in class is no more engaging, no more interactive, and no more motivating than an online class, then why will students go to the trouble of getting out of bed, traveling to your school, and learning at the time and loca-tion of your choosing, when they can learn on their own time wherever they can access WiFi? If your only real value is certification, then you are in trouble when certification can be achieved more easily from other sources.

One of the reasons that change is necessary in schools is that the survival of schools is not guaranteed. One need only look at countless other indus-tries to see how quickly technology has revolutionized, and in some cases destroyed, what appeared to be solid institutions and industries. Educators who think that it's impossible that it could happen to us need to talk to someone who used to be a travel agent or repaired transistor radios and TVs.

Quality versus accountability. One of the unfortunate trends that has emerged in North American education, and particularly in the United States, is an extreme focus on accountability, which implies that if teachers and administrators just do their job properly, then students will do well on standardized tests, which will somehow translate into future success. Unfortunately, this hasn't really worked out as planned. The accountability line of reasoning posits that if you simply do more of what you are currently doing with a narrower focus, and add additional pressure, then you will get what you want: better quality. Instead, more accountability has led to the standardization of the student experience, with little room to honor student individuality and build on their unique strengths; cheating; a narrowing of the curriculum; the elimination of recess in some districts; extreme pressure on students, teachers, and administrators; and a test-taking gamesmanship that values standardized test performance over meaningful learning, student engagement, and the maximization of student potential.

Such an intense focus on testing does not offer students the opportunity to explore complexity and the inherent messiness of learning and overlooks the critical skills—collaboration, problem solving, cultural sensitivity, tenacity, and more—that today's workplaces flag as essential to the continually evolving global workplace. It has negatively affected the quality of the system, producing high school graduates who are ill-equipped to handle the challenges that follow high school. In fact, many graduates have a shockingly high chance of dropping out of college in their first year. A recent study showed that not only is the college completion rate currently an abysmal 52.9 percent in the United States, it's also dropping (Shapiro et al., 2015).

The industry-inspired production line model underlies many of the current trends in accountability. Business's intense focus on metrics has been transferred into the educational sphere, with problematic results: The overly simplistic application of these metrics has punished students, schools, and administrators in neighborhoods with low socioeconomic status for not measuring up. It has also resulted in minimal meaningful change. Metrics themselves are not a bad idea, but what we measure and how we measure is crucial. Using multiple-choice tests, bringing negative attention to communities that are already struggling, and embarrassing rather than supporting them is bound to fail our students. A school is not a branch plant that is having difficulty maintaining profitability. It's an incubator for the future.

It's not an accident that some of the best education systems in the world have placed far less focus on superficial accountability and far more focus on delivering high-quality learning experiences (by contrast, e.g., Norwegian students take a single, standardized test at the age of 16). The central issue is what is best for students and how to build the learning around them rather than building them into the learning.

Testing-focused education often creates schools where success is as much about gaming the system as it is about authentic, meaningful learning. To win the game, students have developed superficial strategies that distance them from meaningful learning, such as listening just enough in class to reproduce the material on a test.

So, what can be gleaned from these strategies? What do they tell us about the system and what they implicitly and explicitly teach students? They show us that learning remains largely a passive experience that isn't tied to student interests, an emphasis on rote learning and compliance is still commonplace, and true engagement and relationship-building tend to happen in activities that take place outside the classroom.

School Doesn't Always Work for Teachers, Either

There are a lot of teachers who are struggling. The job is incredibly complex and demanding. It's also a profession that can be driven as much by guilt as by inspiration: Am I doing the best I can for my students? Are they learning as much as they can? Could I have made more of a difference? Is my class interesting? Am I the teacher that I dreamed I would be when I entered the profession? Many teachers are their own harshest critics. Unfortunately, the result is that many feel they can never work hard enough, be creative enough, or stay on top of all the latest trends and technologies. It's also true that many struggle to stay out of a rut, bored themselves with the daily, unending demands of school. Teachers

- Often work harder than their students;
- Feel like they have to stand on their heads to make their lessons consistently interesting;
- Struggle to figure out why students aren't making more progress;
- Feel the pressure of coaxing students to do well on standardized tests;
- Are expected to implement an endless array of top-down reforms;
- Are then blamed when the reforms don't work; and

- Often go home tired, underappreciated, and frustrated that they can't get their students to where they want them.

Why Is Change So Hard to Come By?

None of the problems with the education system are the result of purposeful malice or ill will. Most of the educators I know are selfless, thoughtful, caring, and hardworking. So why is the system so difficult to change? Why do most of the best intentions fall by the wayside? Education systems have the impressive ability to perpetuate themselves because we are all a product of the system, and those who later go on to work in education are reticent to change a system they know and understand so well.

It doesn't have to be this way. School doesn't have to be boring; it's something I've joked about at staff meetings: "You know, it's not actually written anywhere that school has to be boring for students and teachers. If you are in the middle of a lesson and your students look bored, and you feel bored yourself, start doing something else—immediately." School can be exciting. It can be inspiring. It can be fulfilling. It can be a place where the love of learning is both celebrated and actively promoted. The challenge is to abandon our antiquated views of what school *has* to be and embrace a new concept of what it really *should* be by redefining our relationships with our students, creating opportunities for leadership, and creating the circumstances that will enhance learning for all students.

The key is not to expect the teacher to provide all of this, which is both unfair and unrealistic, but rather to structure classrooms driven by student interests, creativity, and passion, creating a learning environment that is better for both students *and* teachers.

Ideas That Can Show Us the Way

Reimagining what school can and should look like is no easy task. Trying to figure out what's needed in school starts with a bigger question about the overall direction we should take, the skills and knowledge students need to get there, and a deeper analysis of what is currently taking place in schools. The following writers and thinkers—Tony Wagner, Carol Dweck, and Daniel Pink—all have insights that serve as the underlying foundations of this book's approach to empowering students with authentic, real-world learning.

Survival Skills

When we start to reflect on a shift in the direction in the classroom, it's important to keep the end goal in mind: What should students learn to be successful during their school year, and more important, what should they be learning to promote success *after* school? In response to his observation that we have an obsolete system of schooling, Tony Wagner (2008), after years of research, has identified what he refers to as *survival skills* for students in the 21st century:

- Critical thinking and problem solving
- Collaboration across networks and leading by influence
- Agility and adaptability
- Initiative and entrepreneurship
- Effective oral and written communication
- Accessing and analyzing information
- Curiosity and imagination

If we were to build an education system from the ground up that was designed to maximize these skills, it would likely not look much like a traditional school. For one thing, Wagner's list requires students working in real-world terms; the notion of agility and adaptability is almost completely absent in a typical classroom. Even pieces like curiosity and imagination are often in very short supply. Second, many of the skills require students to work together on meaningful projects; in a traditional classroom, students are put together to work on a math problem or class project, but often discussion is dominated by the teacher without the level of collaboration needed to foster the skills. In real terms, it is likely that in the majority of classrooms, the teacher will spend more time using these skills than the students will over the course of the year.

Growth Mindset

Underlying the ability to develop the agility and adaptability that Wagner references is the ability to embrace change. Psychologist Carol Dweck has become well known in educational circles for her recognition of the importance of mindsets. Dweck believes that we can encourage students to develop either *growth mindsets* or *fixed mindsets.*

A growth mindset is one where we believe that our "intelligence or personality is something you can develop"; a fixed mindset is one where we believe they are a "fixed, deep-seated trait" (Dweck, 2006, p. 4). Thus, seeing learning as an ongoing process and not a series of judgments by a teacher is crucial to both future success and self-esteem. It is also not a coincidence that teachers with a growth mindset are more effective because they "set high standards for all their students, not just the ones who are already achieving" (p. 200). They teach their students to "love learning. To eventually learn and think for themselves. And to work hard on the fundamentals" (p. 202).

It's interesting to note that the fixed mindset is also a mindset most frequently associated with high school dropouts, who are less likely to believe they have control of their destinies than their graduating counterparts.

Drive

Student engagement in learning is another important factor to consider. Returning to Pink's *Drive*, he observes, for example, that a website like Wikipedia has required thousands of hours of volunteer effort that is not explained by traditional economics because the majority of the work has been done for free by an army of dedicated volunteers. Basic economic theory can't explain projects like Wikipedia because it's not clear what the tangible gain is for the participants. After extensive research, he concludes that the three factors that motivate people (beyond basic biological and economic need) are the following:

- Autonomy (the ability to have control over what one is doing),
- Mastery (the enjoyment that comes from doing something that we are good at), and
- Purpose (the ability to find intrinsic value in what we do) (Pink, 2009).

Again, these factors tend to be in short supply in a traditional classroom that mostly relies on the external reward of grades.

Whose School Is It?

Two important questions are the extent to which students have input into their schools and their education, and what they are fundamentally looking for from their school. Returning to Wagner's work, he states:

The overwhelming majority of students today want learning to be active, not passive. They want to be challenged to think and to solve problems that do not have easy solutions. They want to know *why* they are being asked to learn something. They want learning to be an end itself—rather than a means to the end of boosting test scores or a stepping stone to the next stage of life. They want more opportunities for creativity and self-expression. Finally, they want adults to relate to them on a more equal level. (Wagner, 2008, pp. 199–200)

This is a marked departure from the goals of the adults who created our traditional system.

This lack of student agency is further reflected in the writings of Adam Fletcher (2015), working from the work of Roger Hart for UNICEF, who created a ladder of student participation in school. In many instances, students are given token levels of participation in school leadership rather than genuine input. In his Ladder of Student Involvement in Figure 1.1, the highest rungs involve children making decisions and acting as real partners with adults.

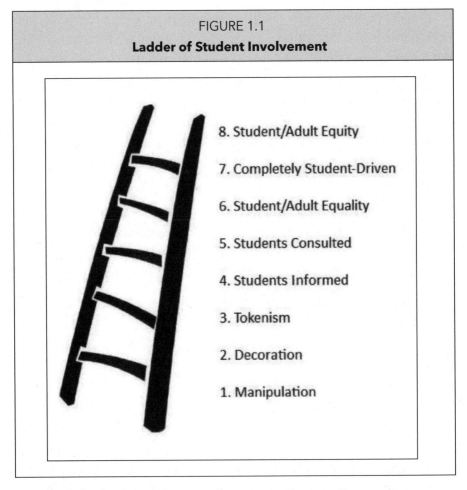

FIGURE 1.1
Ladder of Student Involvement

8. Student/Adult Equity

7. Completely Student-Driven

6. Student/Adult Equality

5. Students Consulted

4. Students Informed

3. Tokenism

2. Decoration

1. Manipulation

Source: From *Meaningful School Involvement: Guide to Students as Partners in School Change,* by A. Fletcher, p. 7. Copyright 2015 by Adam Fletcher. Reprinted with permission.

The concept is both interesting and provocative because, like the skills proposed by Wagner and the sources of motivation provided by Pink, what Fletcher is proposing looks starkly different from a traditional school structure. So how do we begin to create a context in schools where students are active participants, motivated, and learning the skills they need for a constantly evolving world?

Uniting in a Cohesive Vision: Six Steps to Foster Real-World Learning

What emerges from all of these challenges is the need for a school system that intentionally places students at the center, not in a cursory way but in a way in which students have the opportunity to genuinely learn and practice the skills they will need to be successful; be energized to do so through the motivation of autonomy, mastery, and purpose; have the voice and authority in the school to make all of this happen; and develop a mindset that they can continue to grow, both inside and outside school, into lifelong learners.

What's energizing about this vision is a recognition that real improvement does not require complicated theoretical approaches or copious resources. Every single school has the resources required—they just need to start *really* listening to their students and letting them take the lead.

Before we jump in, it's worth pointing out two important things about the steps and their relationship to each other. First, the steps (see Figure 1.2) are open-ended, in part because the specifics of a teaching assignment can look quite different. The job of a grade 1 classroom teacher, for example, looks quite different from that of a senior high school computer teacher. This also means that the use of the steps and strategies—how often they are used and how they are used—is going to shift depending on the developmental stage of the students. Having said that, all the steps and strategies are useful throughout the range of student education experience, even if they grow and change as students get older. What they look like in your classroom depends on you, your students, and your context.

The steps are broad enough that it is possible to start with one or two and to begin to experiment with them in limited ways in your classroom, and there are suggestions on how to do so in each chapter. It is neither necessary nor advisable to throw out everything you are doing in order to begin to play with these ideas. I've identified beginner steps and more advanced steps to help you figure out where to start.

FIGURE 1.2		
Six Steps to Foster Real-World Learning		
Step	**The Big Ideas**	**Activation Questions**
1. Make Meaning Central to Student Work	Start with meaning. Provide the opportunity *and* motivation to lead. Make learning a challenge. Connect student learning to the real world. Use backward design to get to where you want to go.	To what extent do your students find the day-to-day work they do in school meaningful? How frequently do your students want to continue with their learning even after the bell has rung? As a teacher, how would you measure the level of engagement of *all* the students in your class?
2. Contextualize the Curriculum	View the curriculum as a tool. Make the *why* explicit. Be flexible.	Do you see the curriculum as a checklist or a toolbox? How often do you refer to "covering" the curriculum? When your students ask you, "Why are we learning this?" how satisfactory a response are you able to give them?
3. Create Space to Learn	Make room for active learners. Create space to fail. Change the environment to change the learner. Resource student work appropriately. Model lifelong learning.	How much of your school day is driven by student interest and initiative? To what extent do you use choice, and accept student suggestions, as a part of your teaching practice? How are you honoring the learning that students are doing outside school in the classroom? What are you doing to ensure that students can see themselves reflected in your classroom?

Step	The Big Ideas	Activation Questions
4. Connect Student Work to the Community	Form community partnerships. Give students an audience. Recognize the social nature of learning. Embrace competition. Take students into the community.	How many community partners are you currently working with? To what extent are you taking advantage of the resources located in your neighborhood to enhance student learning? How frequently do you take students into the community or bring the community into the classroom?
5. Follow the (Student) Leaders	Remember that students are constantly learning. Default to yes. Avoid riding to the rescue. Involve students in curricular decisions. Embrace your changing role.	How much of the instructional time in your class is directed by students' initiative? When giving students a task, how much time will you leave them to struggle with a problem before you intervene? To what extent are your students aware of the curriculum and involved in discussions about how best to show their learning?
6. Reenvision Feedback and Evaluation	Start with meaning. Co-create assessment criteria and learning goals. Provide more feedback and less evaluation. Enjoy grading.	How frequently do you provide students formative feedback as opposed to evaluations of their work? What evidence do you have that students are clearly learning and improving through the feedback and evaluation you are providing? How much time do you spend grading at home versus conferencing with students during class time?

All that's required is an open mind, a willingness to experiment, and a belief that school can be better.

Make Meaning Central to Student Work

Step 1: Make Meaning Central to Student Work

The Big Ideas

- Start with meaning.
- Provide the opportunity *and* motivation to lead.
- Make learning a challenge.
- Connect student learning to the real world.
- Use backward design to get to where you want to go.

Activation Questions

To what extent do your students find the day-to-day work they do in school meaningful?

How frequently do your students want to continue with their learning even after the bell has rung?

As a teacher, how would you measure the level of engagement of *all* the students in your class?

A few years ago, I was both vice principal and half-time grade 7 teacher at a school in Ontario close to the south branch of the Rideau River. My two grade 7 teaching partners—

Henriette Prosper and Heather Mahaffey—and I worked to build the school year around a large environmental project.

On the first day of school, we issued the students the following challenge: "Reduce the environmental footprint of the school and the community." There were plenty of quizzical looks. Students were not accustomed to being given a large challenge on the first day of school, and some were not even clear exactly what it meant. "Wait, what's an environmental footprint?" one of the boys asked, looking mildly panicked. As we started to discuss it, and they understood how large the challenge was, they looked skeptical about structuring a school year this way and their ability to make it happen. The questions started to flow: "How are we going to affect the whole school?" "What can we do to make this happen?" "How can you possibly expect us to change the community?" You know we're only in grade 7, right?" The students looked both miffed and curious. Clearly, this year was going to be different, and they weren't sure how to feel about it.

It was the best year I ever spent in a classroom (as it was for many of the students, too, we learned from feedback at the end of the year). Here is what we learned from the experience.

Start with Meaning

As referenced earlier, Daniel Pink (2009) argues that outside of basic biology and economics, what drives us is autonomy, mastery, and purpose. Unfortunately, the purpose of school, beyond the rather superficial goal of getting good grades and moving on, is not often apparent to students.

Students faced with a pile of handouts to complete are right to ask about the purpose of the work they are doing. If the central goal is learning, is this really the best methodology? At some point, we need to step back and analyze the learning and tasks that we are giving students by asking ourselves the following questions:

- Does this have relevance outside the context of school?
- Is this something I would want to do myself?
- Do the students find meaning and purpose in the work?

One challenge is that we don't always find the meaning in the curriculum directly. Yes, students need to learn to read and write, but what are they reading and writing *about?* Is it meaningful to them beyond "This assignment is due on Thursday"?

In the South Branch environmental project, we spent the first several weeks of school getting the students fired up about a range of concerns, such as the giant patches of floating plastic garbage affecting the worlds' oceans and coastlines. We also had frank conversations about the fact that school often asked them to be passive followers but that we wanted them to be active leaders. We fired up their passion for the natural world by reading a novel with environmental themes, regularly looking at newspaper and magazine articles about the environment, engaging them in conversations about humans and our relationship with the planet and complex environmental issues, and looking at examples of people taking action to make the environment better. We encouraged them to think creatively about the problems they were wrestling with, spent more time providing formative feedback on their work, and de-emphasized grades in the class. We toured the local water filtration plant as well as garbage and recycling facilities. We also talked about leadership, teamwork, and the roles that different people play on teams.

The students were broken into groups (composting, recycling, energy efficiency, etc.) and started a web page. After looking at ways to create a persuasive environmental message, they held a kickoff assembly in the gym with the rest of the school to educate, encourage, and inspire the other classes to change their actions. For example, the composting group put bins in every class, taught the younger students what went in them, emptied and cleaned the bins regularly, and then weighed and charted the amount of material they were successfully diverting from the landfill. We examined environmental messaging in the media and spoke about what they thought worked and didn't work when trying to get people on side with a goal; they saw how using humor and having fun could be motivating. So, to get classes motivated, they held fundraisers that were used to fund friendly competitions. For example, classes could win an ice cream party for doing the most in the school to reduce their waste.

We worked hard to give context to everything we taught. Here are some examples:

When we talked about persuasive writing, we had students write and submit environmental grant applications to a national contest. The result? The students were awarded $2,000, which they used to purchase improved composting equipment and additional shade trees for the yard, after doing some research and visiting a local tree farm to find out which species would be the best fit. They also planted the trees themselves (and the tree farm delivered for free and sold to the students at cost when they found out what they were doing).

When we had students write newspaper articles, we pitched the idea of running a series of articles to the local newspaper about how community members could make positive changes at home. They loved the concept and sent a reporter to talk to the classes about what it's like to write for a paper. Every group had to submit an article to the newspaper on a deadline, including their photos and at least one paragraph written by each member of the group, because we wanted them all to be published writers. The answer to the question "Why do we have to spend time editing our articles?" was "Because 30,000 people are going to read it and your name and photo will be attached to the work." It was never so easy to get students to participate in a writing conference with us and then follow up diligently with fixing their mistakes.

In math, work on data management focused on using and representing the data the students themselves were collecting on the school's reduction of garbage or use of electricity. The students then used the data to reinforce their arguments in grant applications and articles.

Students worked on effective oral communication to prepare them for whole-school assemblies that they ran. We spoke extensively about audience, how to create engagement and excitement, being concise, and speaking clearly for the audience to hear so that they could get the rest of the school on board with their goals. Students ran upbeat assemblies with game shows and prizes to get other students excited. They could then evaluate their effectiveness through the progress in the data they were collecting.

The inherent meaningfulness of the environmental program is what drove the students, not the grades. Meaning is not some hoped-for outcome at the end of the process; it is where the process begins. Deliberately creating a useful, meaningful, and engaging context for the work will drive everything that follows. As the year went on, students less and less frequently asked the dreaded question "Why are we doing this?" because we answered the question right up front: "We are going to learn about ecosystems because we need to understand how humans and the natural world interact if we're going to make our project a success."

Where Do I Begin?

While making meaning central to the work of your classroom can seem daunting, opportunities emerge daily.

Start with the students. What are your students interested in? What does their experience of the world look like? What do they ask questions about? How often have you had a sidebar conversation where one student asks you about something not related to what you are currently doing in class, and your response leads to more and more questions, creating a more energetic classroom? At some point we tend to stop the conversation to get back to the lesson, and the energy quickly dissipates. Next time this happens, write the issue down and take some time to start developing a plan with the students. Ask them how to connect what you are doing in class to the issue or problem that has them fired up.

For example, during one discussion that year, I recall mentioning something to students about debt and compound interest. The students lamented that school didn't teach them "any of that important stuff," meaning money management and personal finances. A few days later we pulled up an online loan calculator in math class and ran some scenarios to show how compound interest could hurt (credit cards) and help them (savings). They were astounded at the fact that, starting as young as they were, they could be millionaires by the time they retired with reasonable weekly savings. Remember, we don't have to do all the hard work of creativity and innovation on our own; in fact, it's both easier and better when the students are involved, and we can often find connections between what they want to learn and what we have to teach. We just need to be flexible.

Here are some other ways that we can start with students.

Begin the year with a questionnaire or interest survey. Take time to find out what students are interested in before getting too far into the year.

Maintain a question board in the classroom. Part of creating a meaningful classroom comes from stoking students' natural curiosity and questioning. Contrast the way a 3-year-old asks "Why?" endlessly to build an understanding of cause and effect with the much more limited question asking of many senior high school students. Stoking curiosity is crucial to building meaning. Pulling a particularly good question off the board and asking students how it could be incorporated into your collective learning is a powerful message about their interests and their role in the classroom as active participants.

Connect their world with the larger world around them. Sometimes the role of the teacher is to act as a bridge builder. In our case in South Branch, students' interest in technology made it natural to teach them how to create a wiki and build a website as part of our environmental project and to give them a platform for publishing their work. Creative teachers, seeing their students' interest in the game Minecraft (a virtual world with endless building blocks that can be used to build anything students can imagine), have engaged students in creating settings from novels they were reading, exploring models of historical buildings (e.g., the Globe Theatre in London), writing about characters they've created, building a model of the water cycle, or replicating a historical battlefield. Meaning can be made on many platforms, so be open to working in a platform that students are already interested in and use.

Don't shy away from big ideas. Issues that resonate in the world are a good place to start, even if you are going to work on the issue in a local context. The environment, human rights, poverty, justice, and equity are all good potential starting points.

Engaging students in work that is important is crucial to increased engagement and deeper learning. Consider these questions as you begin your work:

- What work are students currently doing that they would consider meaningful? What work would still be meaningful to them a month from now? A year from now?
- From your own experience: How much of the learning do you remember from when you were in school? What has stuck with you and why?

It's amazing to think about how few specifics most of us remember from our school learning. The chances are that you remember learning that was exciting, interesting, challenging, and relevant to you.

Find ways to connect these big issues to your context. Most big issues can be worked on anywhere, but they might look different depending on where you are. With the South Branch project, we were in a small town, so getting involved directly with the town made sense. When the children of farmers at S. J. McLeod Public School (K–6) tackled an environmental project in a more rural setting, they worked to bring farmers and environmentalists together to discuss how best to preserve the quality of water in the area. An environmental project with disadvantaged youth from the city of Halifax that saw students growing vegetables and herbs on small urban plots of land, which then turned into a business making and selling salad dressing, is a good example of how environmental issues can be tackled even in an urban setting.

Build understanding. Remember that a certain amount of groundwork may be necessary for building student engagement and success with complex issues. Sometimes students aren't fired up about issues because they simply don't know enough about them. Our classes weren't particularly knowledgeable about the environment before we began, which is why we spent a lot of time at the beginning reading and talking about various issues. This part of the journey looked a little more like traditional teaching, but the difference was that we were providing necessary information and context for the actions they were going to take, not simply preparing them for a test. We also didn't tell students what to think. Presenting students with a newspaper article and video on, for example, the Great Pacific Garbage Patch caused their natural sense of unfairness about the situation to bubble quickly to the surface. It also led to a lot of healthy debate. Equally important, however, was using an approach that considered the complexities of the issue, including our heavy dependence on plastic and how an issue like this could emerge. We weren't trying to make the problems appear less complicated than they were. We wanted students to understand this complexity and still take actions in their community to make positive changes.

Overcoming Obstacles

Here are a few potential problems that could arise and ways that you can avoid them.

Students aren't interested. It is sometimes tempting to start with something that we are passionate about but the students aren't interested in. In some cases, we can educate them to the point that it becomes important to them, too (as referenced above), but in other cases it just isn't meaningful to them. If the students aren't fired up, then it's probably time to step back, have a conversation with them, and look for a spark that you can build on. Again, this might be a time where it's necessary to play the role of bridge builder.

In my own classroom experience, teaching poetry was, at times, a real slog. Getting students to really *work* at a poem, spend enough time digging into it, and understand how it was constructed could be a real challenge. What most students *are* enthusiastic about is music. Looking at poetry thematically, inviting students to bring in music and lyrics where they see connections, and then sharing that work with the class suddenly gave them a newfound respect for poetry and a better understanding of it because it was now connected to something they were passionate about.

Remember that an apparent failure is also a great opportunity to model how important failure is to learning. Think of the positive modeling and open-mindedness involved in a conversation that starts like this: "This isn't working. I thought that this would be of interest to you, but I can see now that it means more to me than it does to you. How do you think we can pivot or change our focus so that we can still touch on these curriculum expectations that I want you to learn in a way that will be interesting to you?" Modeling that you don't get it right all the time, that you recognize that sometimes our ideas don't work, and that when that happens we need to take a step back and change directions might be one of the most powerful, real-world lessons you teach students all year.

Students prefer traditional teaching. Recognize that a certain amount of deprogramming may be required before students fully engage. At the start of the year at South Branch, we spent time talking about the skills and practices that traditional classrooms had encouraged in them that would need to be abandoned if the project were to be a success. This shift was difficult for some students, most notably the ones who generally did well at school. During the course of the year, I occasionally had a bright student say, "Can we please just read a chapter in the textbook and take a test? This project-based stuff is too much thinking and work." To which I would respond with a smile, "I'm terribly sorry that we've done this to you, but learning to problem solve, think on your own, and collaborate is really important." Don't be surprised if you see the same issues, and don't let it throw you off course. Remember, doing something different in class is as much of a learning experience for you as it is for the students, and both will likely experience some growing pains. Be prepared for some pushback when you ask students to wrestle with meaningful content, but also take time to explain to them, and their parents, why you are doing it. At the end of the day, it's very difficult to argue with the need for real meaning.

Students fear that the problem seems too large. Your approach in the classroom needs to be influenced by the students' developmental age and stage. Students at a young age can wrestle with challenging ideas, but it needs to be in a context they can relate to. For example, a primary class is likely not ready for a discussion about the treatment of political prisoners, but they do have a very clearly defined sense of fairness, so your discussion of justice might focus on the school yard (e.g., leaving other students out of the games they are playing or creating rules in their games that are unfair to others). If this goes well, it could be scaled up to talk about fairness for other members of the immediate community.

This is also where some traditional teaching methods can still serve students. As referenced earlier, students don't always know a lot about the world around them, so giving them some foundations about an issue is an important part of the process. The difference in the context of real-world learning is that we are providing them this information because they need it so that *they can take action*. The world is full of challenges and issues that will naturally elicit deeply human responses from students. This education has purpose, which is not often the case when our focus is mainly on covering the curriculum.

Finally, getting work that is at that "just right" level takes some practice, so prepare to be flexible and give yourself a break if it's not exactly right the first time you try it. Like anything, it becomes easier with practice.

Here are some common areas where issues can arise and how you can adjust them appropriately:

- **The size of the problem or project.** If it becomes apparent the problem or project really is too big, take a step back and ask the students to help come up with a plan that will address the initial steps with the time and resources available. Again, it's great modeling to say to students, "I think we've bitten off more than we can chew. Do you agree? Let's brainstorm how to make this more manageable so that we can accomplish something we can all feel good about in the next three weeks." Similarly, if the problem is too small, we can engage students by asking them what the next logical steps are and how can we use the time remaining to maximum efficiency.

- **The issue itself is too complex.** If you are feeling that students are really struggling to understand the issue that you've brought them, it's time to listen. Have individual conversations with students in the class and ask them the following questions: "Tell me what you understand about this issue so far. What questions do you still have? Is there something that has you confused?" The answers to these questions will tell you a lot about whether the students really understand or not. There's a good chance the answers will also provide you with some ideas about how you can modify your approach or cut off a smaller part of it that will be manageable for the students. Don't feel sheepish about making changes. Adjusting our ideas with the participation of the class is great role modeling.

If we understand that adjusting as we go amounts to good teaching and role modeling, it takes the pressure off having to get things right every time. This is part of the learning process for you and your students. Telling them right up front, "I'm going to try something new with you, and I'm not sure if it's going to work, but I really feel it's worth the risk to try" sends an important message about your own growth mindset. Expect great things; in most cases you will be shocked at how often students exceed expectations. But if not, that's okay, too. It's also part of the learning.

Provide the Opportunity *and* Motivation to Lead

Teacher Shawn Grimes wanted to give students a real challenge to solve. He started a tech club at school to have students learn, with a tech professional, how to design websites. In what he calls a WebSLAM (Student Learning Apprenticeship Model) hackathon, students designed sites for nonprofits in the community. The program has now expanded from its origins in Baltimore to include events in Philadelphia and Columbus, Ohio, with more than 300 students participating and 60 websites designed.

Students have learned to "understand their client's needs, articulate the organization's purpose visually and through text, and work collaboratively with others to get the job done in the limited amount of time available. The value of the real-world skills that the youth have learned . . . is equally matched by the intrinsic motivation that they bring to the job at hand when sitting across the table from a real person whose real need they are in a position to really serve" (Grimes, 2016).

We sometimes get frustrated in education when students are reticent to take responsibility for their own learning or to take on leadership roles; it's also frustrating when they take on the role and make a lackluster effort. Sometimes it's necessary to take a step back and reflect on what we are asking them to do and our expectations.

The opportunity for genuine leadership, driven by the desire to complete meaningful work, is important. Genuine leadership is where there is a real purpose for the leadership and a real-world goal to accomplish. For example, if students are too closely following a teacher's directions, then they aren't really leading at all. Directing a student to lead a group of others by completing a step-by-step, teacher-provided assignment may be a starting point, but it is not the same as challenging students as a group to alter the environmental behavior of the rest of the school, as reflected in the example from South Branch.

It's difficult to be an effective leader if

- You don't really believe in the importance of what you are doing.
- The scope of your leadership has been too tightly defined.
- Those you are supposed to be leading are not motivated to follow because they don't see the purpose of what they are doing either.

A sense of shared purpose and a passion for what you are doing is crucial to genuine leadership opportunities, as is the opportunity to make meaningful decisions and have real input. Within the group there is an important need to be cohesive, while also recognizing the autonomy of group members: being micromanaged is highly demotivating. As adults, we have likely run into micromanaging leaders at some point in our lives and are familiar with how they foster feelings of mistrust and limit the value of collaboration and input from the broader group.

The challenge for teachers is to find a rallying point for students that will make them want to take up the challenge of leading and collaborating. That's not to say that this doesn't sometimes require a little work. At South Branch, we spent time exposing students to a variety of environmental disasters at the beginning of the year. While many students had some environmental awareness before we started, by educating them about a wide variety of fairly shocking environmental violations, we stoked their passion for helping. They evaluated examples of environmental media on their effectiveness and used this information to create their own persuasive messaging. A history teacher might need to find particular stories, characters, or issues from history that students can get excited about or connect current events to historical causes. A biology teacher might need to get students fired up about a controversial issue like genetically modified food or a local endangered species. An elementary teacher might need to get students excited about reading and writing by demonstrating the power of publishing and sharing their ideas widely using social media. Remember, motivation can be fostered. This is where a teacher's passion and knowledge can be invaluable. Getting students excited about their learning is key and will often be the first step in the action process.

It's also important that there is enough space in the work for students to find themselves in it. Projects that involve teams with multiple roles will tend to meet the needs of more students. For example, a team that has a tech lead, a public speaker, a designer, and a project manager will help students (1) define their unique role on the team and (2) recognize the benefit of working with other people with a range of interests, skills, and experiences to achieve their shared goal. Too often, we turn students off group work with assignments that don't need a group to complete them before rewarding some students for work they didn't do or punishing others because their classmates haven't been pulling their weight.

Take, for example, students who are asked to work in a group to complete a poster to discourage students from taking up smoking. One or two students in the group quickly take the lead and begin to sketch something out. The other two students, having difficulty getting involved because their peers are not listening to their ideas, begin to lose interest and quickly get off task. The two students doing the work are upset at the end because they did all the work and the other two didn't help; further, they feel it's unfair that all the students received the same grade when their efforts and accomplishments were clearly not the same. The two that were left out are equally dissatisfied because the poster doesn't represent them, they have no sense of ownership, and they found the whole thing boring because they were left out.

Distinct roles, playing to a range of strengths, makes group work important because the central task can't be achieved without every group member's dedication and talents. Individualized feedback and grading from the teacher validate the work of each student and increase their sense of accountability to the group; no one is permitted to ride the coattails of others. We'll talk more about the importance of space for learning in Chapter 4.

Where Do I Begin?

It's important that we make space for both opportunity and motivation.

Start with student interest and talents. As you begin to explore the issue, what talents and opportunities are present in your class that could help direct the work? In the South Branch project, we saw students take on multiple roles that connected with their personal talents and interests: Students with a passion for computers or social media took the lead in the design of their wiki; students who were effective public speakers became the official spokespeople for their group; students who liked to work with their hands assembled composting bins for the schoolyard; those who were strong writers became the student editors for their groups. Consider the Venn diagram in Figure 2.1.

The best projects take place somewhere in the middle—those projects that combine a big idea and curricular expectations with the talents and interests of the students themselves, as well as the opportunities available in the local context.

Leave room for student input. We will discuss the importance of space in more detail later in the book (Chapter 4), but it is important that the project is well structured, while leaving adequate space for individual input. Conferencing regularly with students is vital. Here are some critical questions:

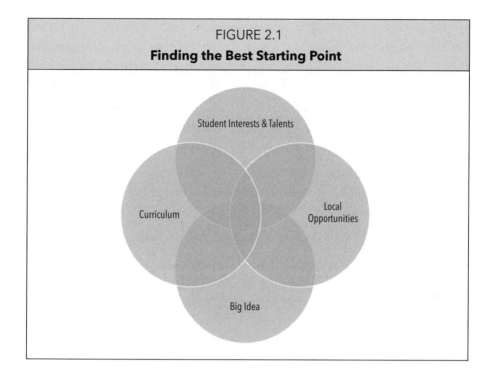

FIGURE 2.1
Finding the Best Starting Point

Student Interests & Talents

Curriculum

Local Opportunities

Big Idea

- How do you feel the project is currently going? Can you give me examples of things that are going well and things that need work?
- Tell me about your role in the work.
- How do you think you are working as a team?
- What are the team's next steps?
- What are your personal next steps?

Note the focus on both the team and the individual work. It's critical to ensure that the team is on the same page and that each individual sees the purpose in the work. This is not about complying with teacher directions.

As Daniel Pink notes, if we are looking for compliance from students, we can only get one of two responses: they will either comply or defy. Neither of these are desirable when we are trying to provide opportunity and motivation to lead. Pink states that "we don't want defiant kids, but we also don't want compliant kids. We want kids who are engaged. If you truly want to engage kids, you have to pull back on control and create the conditions in which they can tap their own inner motivations" (Azzam, 2014).

This is why an appropriate degree of student autonomy needs to be built into the work.

Be flexible. Opportunities will arise as the work continues. If students are bringing forward new ideas, it's important to give them a fair hearing. That's not to say that all ideas are worth pursuing; some may not be possible within the time and scope you have available. However, rather than simply saying either yes or no, it would be wise to establish with the students some criteria to determine whether you will collectively pursue an idea. This can be done early in the process and will provide a sense of fairness to the evaluation of ideas that emerge.

Early in the South Branch project, we used some of these questions when considering ideas:

- Is it safe (e.g., physical safety, online safety)?
- Can it be done within budget?
- Can it be done within the timelines we have?
- Will it have a demonstrable, clear, and positive effect on the work?
- Are there connections to the curriculum?

With some clear questions or criteria to evaluate ideas, the decision about whether to proceed or not was not personal but pragmatic. Some ideas might need to be altered because, for example, students running a fundraiser hadn't considered food allergies. In other cases, ideas were deemed to be just a little too ambitious (e.g., involving the whole district in their work) but could be considered down the road if all the other goals had been accomplished.

As a general rule, the goal is to say yes as much as possible, but if you have to say no, then couching the response with specific reasons for why it's not possible makes the experience less negative. Often, you can suggest an alternative that meets students halfway.

Overcoming Obstacles

Here are some of the common problems you might experience and some ways to address them.

Students are not taking advantage of the opportunity to lead. This can be a result of years of traditional schooling where students have been conditioned to follow rather than lead. They may need some help kicking their old habits. Spending time talking about leadership and, better yet, taking students through leadership exercises can be a good place to start. In the case of the South Branch project, we took an overnight trip to a leadership camp early in the school year to get students started down this road. Of course, this may not be possible in some schools, but a quick web search will reveal dozens of exercises that can be done right in the classroom.

It's also crucial that students have a clear sense of what leadership can look like and why it's important. Clear yet flexible expectations are key. Look at examples of leadership, talk to them about leaders that inspire them, and help them understand the wide range of ways that leadership can manifest itself. Quieter students, for example, need to understand the value and nature of quiet leadership, which looks different but is equally important because leadership is not always about being extroverted and delivering speeches. Introverted students will tend to spend more time focused on accomplishing specific goals and reflecting on solutions to more complex challenges than their more extroverted classmates. They may also develop deeper connections with group members because they will be more likely to spend more time listening to their peers. Effective teams need a balance of extroverted and introverted leaders. Having said that, it's also important that students learn to be effective followers. The world needs dedicated teammates to support important work. Every student should have a chance to play both roles.

It's not clear whether all the students have leadership capacity. This largely relates to the last point. It's important that teachers clarify for themselves all the different forms effective leadership can take. Check your assumptions and ask yourself exactly how you define leadership. Inherent in this work is the belief that all students are capable of learning and that they all have potential that has not been fully maximized. Are all students capable of getting up in front of a group to deliver a rousing speech? Perhaps not, but then that's a fairly narrow view of leadership.

Make Learning a Challenge

One way to generate excitement is to frame a challenge for students. Making the challenge ambitious and large in scope generates interest, motivation, and a little bit of trepidation, which can be helpful. This slight sense of discomfort is important because it means that students are being stretched; it also means that more and deeper learning is likely to take place. When school is too comfortable, it is not preparing students for a complicated world full of uncertainty and nuance. We want students to learn to be comfortable with a certain amount of discomfort. Think of major accomplishments in your own life. There's a very good chance they didn't happen when you were playing it entirely safe.

The other advantage of issuing a challenge is that, by definition, it requires an active response. Challenges require students to use their learning to *accomplish* something. They also serve to expand students' boundaries in a very important way.

Importantly, challenges don't have answers. Often in schools, the end of the process is an answer that is right or wrong, which reinforces the position of the teachers as the fount of all knowledge and makes students less likely to participate for fear of getting the answer wrong. When we look at the work that students will do as they get older, there is seldom a right or wrong answer awaiting them. There are better ways and worse ways, effective ways and ineffective ways, but determining whether something is working or not requires us to step back objectively and figure it out for ourselves. Learning to do this comes with experience. In this structure, the teacher's job is not to hold the right answer but to ask the right questions to prompt student reflection:

- How do you feel this is working or not working? What is your evidence for that?
- What other resources could help you to accomplish your goals?
- Is there another way to do this?
- If you are feeling stuck, is there a way that you can take a step back and work your way *around* the problem?
- Is this your best work? If not, what would make it your best work?

The questions that drive the teacher's guidance are largely the same questions we want students to ask themselves as they get older and learn to problem solve and persevere. It's no accident that they are also the same questions that effective teachers regularly ask themselves. In other words, open-ended challenges that don't have answers are a metaphor for adult life. How you tackle these open-ended challenges, what mindset you bring to them, what skills and experiences you have, and what decisions you make will ultimately determine your success and satisfaction.

At South Branch, we laid out a challenge that students initially had a hard time grasping and felt was impossible. While bringing them to a deeper understanding of some of the underlying issues was a crucial first step, it was the open-endedness of the challenge that ultimately made it so engaging. There is no obvious recipe for reducing a school's environmental footprint, and for some students this was quite unnerving. School was not supposed to work that way. But they were beginning to learn that life is a challenge, so learning should be one, too.

Where Do I Begin?

Here are some important considerations when issuing a challenge to your students.

Create challenges that are open-ended. Keeping challenges open-ended is crucial to increasing student engagement. This is a difficult one for many teachers. It requires that the teacher take on the role of co-pilot rather than pilot. The more limitations we put on students, the less they invest in the challenge. We have an important role to play as guide, and ensuring that ideas are safe and have a reasonable likelihood of success is important, but remember that failure is a great learning experience, too, and we won't ever find out the real potential of our students if we don't leave them enough room to stretch themselves.

Getting the focus of the challenge just right—in the Goldilocks zone—takes some practice, but Figure 2.2 includes an example of how the challenge at South Branch might have looked if it had been either too focused or too broad.

Ensure that the challenge is worth accomplishing. Is there real purpose in completion of the challenge? In other words, will students have done something significant if they are successful in addressing the challenge? These are crucial questions at the beginning of the work. One of the reasons that students often leave school at the end of the day unsatisfied rather than excited is because the work they were engaged in did not lead to a sense of accomplishment.

Be ambitious. Stretching students' potential increases the payoffs significantly. There's very little satisfaction in accomplishing something that is not difficult. For example, if our South Branch project required students to simply reduce paper consumption in their class, it would have been accomplished quickly and forgotten about shortly after that. By creating an ambitious goal (reducing the environmental footprint of the school and community), we let students know that it would take time and considerable effort. In many cases, traditional ideas can be converted into more meaningful, ambitious challenges by extending them past the walls of the classroom and making them more relevant. Figure 2.3 includes some examples.

FIGURE 2.2 Finding the Goldilocks Zone		
Too Focused	**Just Right**	**Too Broad**
Start a composting program at the school.	Reduce the environmental footprint of the school and the surrounding community.	Save the local environment.
Why? • Students could run a composting program without really understanding why it is important. • Directing a specific action (e.g., start a composting program) doesn't leave students sufficient space to bring their own interests and ideas to the table. • The work is meaningful, but without clear ownership of it, it will not be as satisfying to the students who are enacting a teacher's idea, not their own.	**Why?** • The challenge doesn't tell students what to do; instead, it focuses them on a desirable outcome. Students are provided a *what* to do but not a *how*. • The goal is ambitious and open-ended, allowing lots of room for student input and ideas. • The success of the goal is measurable. • The work is meaningful and provides enough room for student ownership that they can take personal satisfaction from it.	**Why?** • The challenge is impossible; there is a clear line between ambitious and overly ambitious. Ambitious invites students to stretch themselves and their learning; overly ambitious will lead to frustration and inaction. • It doesn't hint at the kinds of actions that students might take nor does it have a potentially measurable outcome. • The work puts too much of the onus on the students and not enough on the teacher.

As you can see in Figure 2.3, the challenges are ambitious but not ridiculously so. All of them invite students to find their own entry to them by being sufficiently open-ended. Some are more directed, but all require students to respond meaningfully and are clearly worth doing.

Overcoming Obstacles

Here are a couple of the roadblocks you might run into when making work a meaningful challenge.

Students fail to complete the challenge. There are two important considerations here: (1) The risk of failure can be lowered through the structure of the challenge, and (2) students' notion of failure can be reshaped so that they understand that it is a crucial part of the learning process.

FIGURE 2.3	
Create Meaningful Challenges	
Traditional Assignment	**Meaningful Challenge**
Create a poster explaining how to reduce global warming.	Reduce the amount of CO_2 our class produces at school and at home.
Write an essay about the civil rights movement.	Develop a walking tour map of locations in our community significant to the civil rights movement and distribute it at local tourist information centers.
Develop a PowerPoint presentation about the importance of clean water.	Clean up a local stream or river. Use social media to promote the event, find community partners to help with your work, and educate the community about the importance of clean water.
Research a famous inventor and do an oral presentation.	Design an invention that could improve the quality of life for someone in your family or neighborhood.
Take a test about the essential elements required in starting a business.	Start a profitable small business by selling a product or service within the school or to the local community. Donate the profits to a favorite charity.

As an example of the first point, the South Branch project was not likely to fail because there were many things students could do to reduce the environmental footprint of the school. For example, if the class had run a litter-less lunch for a week, that would technically have met the first part of the challenge. However, it also wouldn't have been a very gratifying response to such a purposeful challenge. The question was really "How big of an effect can you have on the environmental footprint?" and not whether they would have an impact at all.

As to student understanding of failure, ask students early in the process what it will look like if the project is wildly successful and what it will look like if it's more modestly so. At the end of the process, focusing the discussion on learning is crucial because learning, of course, is the ultimate goal. What they accomplish is important, but what they learn is even more so, and failing is probably the best teacher of all.

As Carol Dweck says:

I started studying how students cope with failure because I under-stood from the start that failure was an incredibly important part of attaining success. And what I found was that some kids really fell apart, but others really become mobilized. They woke up, they said I love a challenge, they said things like I was hoping this would be informative. And I knew that they had a secret, but I wanted to understand. . . . And what I learned is that they . . . understood that their intelligence, their abilities were things that could be developed. (Fleming, 2012)

The fact is that student failure to complete a challenge is both a matter of perspective and based on the erroneous assumption that failure is bad or learning didn't take place, which is simply not true. We'll discuss this idea in more detail in Chapter 4.

Colleagues don't approve, school administration is not invested, and parents are worried. Working with other adults is an important part of the process. People are naturally suspicious of new things. Many of us inadvertently subscribe to confirmation bias, which is to say we focus on and interpret information in ways that support ideas we already believe.

Beyond sharing the ideas in this book, keeping them in the loop and being transparent is important to building trust with administrators, colleagues, and parents. Figure 2.4 offers some tips about how to build support from all three constituencies.

Ultimately, the actions of your students will speak for themselves. Students who are excited about coming to school and can provide detailed explanations about what they are doing and why will be the best ambassadors for this approach. It's difficult to argue with great work.

Connect Student Learning to the Real World

It is not uncommon in educational settings to refer to the real world as a location distinct and separate from the educational world. The real world, according to some, is a place where people are uncaring and life is hard; it is the place where irresponsible students will get their comeuppance. The educational world, by contrast, is insular and protective. Such insularity and the "unreality" of school can be impediments to student engagement. It is difficult to create *real* engagement in an *unreal* world. Hence, a crucial step to reengaging students is bridging the gap between the curriculum and the world that surrounds them.

	FIGURE 2.4	
	Building Support	
Colleagues	**School Administration**	**Parents**
Have an open-door policy and invite colleagues to come and see the work in progress.	**Have an open-door policy** and invite administration to come and see the work in progress.	**Invite them in early.** We invited all of the parents in to explain the project, how we were linking it to the curriculum, and our rationale: "We are doing this to engage your children and deepen their learning." It's not reasonable to expect students to explain this at the dinner table; parents need a chance to hear it directly from the teacher and to ask questions.
Invite colleagues to join. Our work at South Branch was made much easier because we worked in a team of three.	**Again, start early.** Administrators, like teachers, will sometimes need time to think about and reflect on new ideas. By laying the groundwork early, keeping administration in the loop, and seeking their input, you can dramatically reduce the risk of resistance.	
Start early. Big projects can take time to get together. We started our discussion in the previous school year before launching the project in the fall. Colleagues' resistance may be more about needing time to think and plan and not about thinking it's a bad idea.	**Make the curricular links clear.** One area that can make administrators nervous is if they feel like the work is no longer tied to the curriculum, even if they see the work is valuable. Sharing the curricular links and how assessment is being managed is important for accountability. This work is not about abandoning the curriculum; it's about making it purposeful (as we'll discuss in Chapter 3).	**Keep them in the loop.** By sharing students' work online, providing parents updates, and inviting them to come in a see the work being done, we can assure parents that the project is on track, and they can hear directly from the students about their learning.
Answer questions honestly and share what's working and what you're continuing to figure out.		
Partner with other classes to bring colleagues into the work. For example, we invited all the classes in the school to get involved with improving their environmental practices, which allowed us to talk with teachers about what we were doing.		
Don't push too hard. Teachers will tend to come to new ideas when they're ready. Pushing colleagues too hard to join will have the opposite effect.		

The future of schooling relies on the gradual elimination of the artificial border between school and the real world. That's not to say that students in the primary grades should be treated like adults, but it does mean that what they are doing should have meaning. As students get older, the lines between school and the world around it should become increasingly blurred.

The lack of experience in working around problems, going back to the drawing board, looking at problems from a different angle, and ultimately overcoming these obstacles means that many students who run into trouble come to a dead stop, become despondent, and are overwhelmed by anxiety. Unfortunately, this appears to be a growing trend: The National Institute of Mental Health indicates as many as 8 percent of teenagers have an anxiety disorder (2015). Many of us are familiar with bright, hardworking students who seem unable to manage the smallest setback. Learning to make the best out of failures and being able to put them in perspective is vital to their future health and happiness.

At South Branch, the real world was carefully woven into our work. We purposely scheduled class trips (to the water treatment plant, a recycling plant, and a team-building and leadership camp) early in the year to get students literally thinking outside of the box of the classroom.

The work in the local community expanded even further. After calling the local government for information about the municipality's environmental practices, we ended up connected with the region's head of planning, who let us know about a city project that we could help with. The city had a snow dump, where plowed snow from the city was deposited, close to an environmentally sensitive river. The town was moving the snow dump because it was leaking salt (used for melting ice) and asbestos (from car brakes) into the river. They wanted to do something recreational with the land but weren't sure exactly what. The student groups were then challenged to design a park, within a realistic budget provided by the town, that would meet the needs of the residents of the area. Municipal staff came to the school to explain the process for creating projects of this kind and gave the students the actual costs of materials you might find in a park. To carry the project forward, students began interviewing neighbors, visiting and photographing the site, and building scale models of the proposed park. Finally, in full business attire, they formally presented their proposal to the mayor and council with a PowerPoint presentation and the scale models they had built. They even got involved with local media, participating in interviews at their meeting with the mayor and council.

The broader community felt the direct effects of the students' work. The class received donations from people in the community who wanted to encourage them. It wasn't important only within the confines of the classroom or curriculum—it was important to the region, and the issues it raised had meaning for the real world.

Where Do I Begin?

Here are some easy ways to connect student work to the real world.

Form partnerships. The easiest way to connect student learning to the real world is to connect with people and organizations outside the classroom. These could be experts in the area you are working with online, local government, other classrooms or schools, businesses, or nonprofit organizations. The fact is, many people are very interested in the idea of helping schools.

You don't have to be the one to organize all the partnerships. If developmentally appropriate, students themselves can call or connect online with potential partners. The partners might be even more inclined to say yes when they hear from the students directly.

When students in Jeff McMillan and Rich Tamblyn's (2006) Commonwealth Public School class in Brockville, Ontario, were completing independent research projects, they were told to connect with outside experts at the local, national, and international levels. Through this prompt, one student developed a relationship with Environment Canada, and a contact there invited the class to attend an upcoming UN Climate Change Conference. Four students ended up attending, filmed the conference, and edited their work into a short film when they returned. The classes then hosted their own environmental summit at the school where students' work, including the film, was shared. The takeaway? There's no telling where partnerships might take students and their learning.

Take advantage of the internet, especially social media. Most students use some kind of social media, most of the time for strictly social purposes. Meaningful challenges can also be a reason for them to use their networks for learning to look for help from the people they are already connected to. It has never been easier to connect with people from around the world. Help students to see that their media contacts can be used for a lot more than simply sharing photos or updates about their social lives. It's also possible to reach out to experts from all over the world in a near infinite number of specialties. Many of them are more than happy to share their passions with students, and there's no telling where the connection could end up. Consider adding a requirement that students connect with local, national, and international experts when working on research or project ideas that have wide-reaching, global effects. Or the next time students are reading a book by a living author, have them reach out via social media. It will dramatically deepen their learning while also teaching them important lessons about the power of the internet and the global community.

There's also an important role for the curriculum to play in connecting student learning to the real world. We'll talk more about that in the next chapter.

Overcoming Obstacles

Here are some ways to deal with potential issues that might emerge.

Connecting to the real world is proving difficult. If you are having difficulties making a connection, it may be time to go back and take a closer look at the challenge. Is it meaningful? Is there a real purpose for it? If you are relying on traditional structures, or textbooks for that matter, this might be the cause of the problem. Remember, textbooks don't exist in the *real world*—that is, the world outside academia. It's not a question of knowledge but rather what we *do* with the knowledge that is important. A sense of purpose is what moves knowledge from the theoretical to the practical, and it's the practical application that shifts it into a real-world experience. Figure 2.5 includes some examples.

If you can't find ways to connect to the real world, then the chances are the work doesn't have a deeper purpose. You may also be thinking in a way that is too subject specific. One thing to note about Figure 2.5 is that all the real-world concepts require a cross-curricular approach; do not allow the artificial separation of subject areas to impede student learning or to make it more relevant. Another suggestion? Do an internet search to see what kind of work is being done in this area. If the work is purposeful, then someone, somewhere, is working on it.

The community partnership is not working well. It's important to have a clear and honest discussion with potential partners about your expectations: How much time will you spend working together? What are your expectations for each other? What is the process if either side has an issue? Are roles and contact people on all sides clearly defined? Working with people outside the school is not always easy. However, the meaningful connection to the real world for student work, and the amazing results that come from good partnerships, is worth the risk.

FIGURE 2.5 Connecting Learning to the Real World		
Area of Knowledge	**Why Do We Study It?**	**What Can We Do with It in the Real World?**
Biodiversity	To better understand the inter-relatedness of organisms and the world, including our own relationships to them	Work on a plan with a local conservation authority to support a local species at risk.
Historical Research	To better understand our current world, we need to understand where we came from and why the world is the way it is today, and where it might be going tomorrow.	Take a name from a local cemetery headstone, conduct research in partnership with a local archive and museum, and create a product that brings that historical person to life.
Data Analysis	To better understand how numbers can be used to increase our comprehension about complex issues to help us make decisions	Conduct a survey of the student body and staff to come up with a plan to reduce bullying in the school by identifying key locations and times during the school day when it's most likely to take place.

It's also important to remember that community members who don't normally work in schools or with students may need some guidance ahead of time to increase the chances of success. Explain to them where your students are developmentally, what partners can expect from them, and what will (active engagement) and won't (talking for too long) work when partnering with students. For example, in our project, we emphasized with partners that 7th graders could be expected to attend for no more than 20 minutes, at which point they should be engaged with a discussion question or activity. This helped ensure a positive experience for both the students and our partners.

Even with these precautions, sometimes a partnership just does not work out. If that happens, end the partnership amicably and look for another. Take it as an opportunity to speak to students about the reality that sometimes things don't work out, so we need to be realistic about partnerships and progress, treat people professionally, and move on to another partnership if necessary. This is an incredibly valuable lesson for students to learn.

Use Backward Design to Get to Where You Want to Go

One way to provide students with adequate structure, while maintaining the space discussed in the last chapter, is to work backward. By providing students with a specific and meaningful end point, the journey to that point can be negotiated. Differentiation becomes about the degree to which the journey may by scaffolded, that is, the degree to which you as the teacher need to help a student move along the journey. In each case, the amount of assistance given should be the least amount of assistance required to achieve the final goal. By having students working in collaboration, the teams themselves will, through their collective creativity and ability to problem solve, work out many of the issues on their own. The role of the teacher is more often about asking the right question ("Is there another way you can do this?") than providing direction ("This is what you should do next").

Using a backward design model also reinforces the reality of the task, in that this is the way that the real world works. There is typically some larger goal to which most adult work is attached: make a profitable product, raise a certain amount of money, and so on. The what and sometimes the why are usually clear, but the how is not always well defined. Students need to learn to be comfortable with this open-endedness. It's no different for teachers: There is nothing less inspiring than teaching from a teacher's handbook that mechanically covers the curriculum and provides a day-by-day script. A textbook may be a jumping-off point, but it's not the entire course. Like so many things in education, as go the students, so goes the teacher. You need a meaningful end goal as much as your students do.

We used backward design to organize our work at South Branch. Collaborating during the month of June and just before school started, my two colleagues and I built the basic plan by cutting up a printout of the overall curriculum expectations for the year and placing the strips on a table. As we talked and brainstormed about environmental connections, we moved the curriculum expectations into groups. We then laid them out over the 10 months of the school year, teaching the skills and knowledge in the curriculum when it was required to support the project, not in the order they appeared in the textbook. For example, in math we covered ratio and rate in the lead-up to the students building the scale models that went on display at City Hall. While there were expectations that did not fit well (which we simply ended up teaching in a more traditional format), we were able to integrate much of the curriculum in a meaningful way.

It's also important to realize that while developing a project, it is frequently necessary to jump back and forth between the three crucial elements: the goal of the project, the curriculum, and student interests and abilities. The strategy we used with the South Branch project of cutting up and laying the curriculum expectations on the table was a simple way to shape the structure of the project, plan a month-by-month calendar, and effectively lay out timelines and deadlines for the students. It also allowed us to find more curriculum connections than we originally estimated while simultaneously giving us additional project ideas by borrowing from the skills and knowledge in the curriculum (discussed in the next chapter).

Where Do I Begin?

Here are some suggestions about how to get started.

Working backward, begin to tease out what will be required to complete the challenge. Once you have the challenge worked out, consider these universal questions both at the beginning and throughout the challenge:

- What work on leadership will we need to do before we begin?
- What kind of information and skills will students need to accomplish the task?
- How can we connect the project to the curriculum?
- What resources might we require to complete the task?
- What partnerships can we form, both inside and outside the school, to help make the challenge a reality?
- Who should we be talking to?

Be ready to course correct. Continuing to ask the questions throughout is vital to taking advantages of the opportunities that might emerge. When we initially set out on our environmental challenge, the project to design the riverside park was not part of our consideration. The opportunity only presented itself after discussions with the municipality. Our adaptable approach allowed us to take full advantage of the amazing opportunity. There's a good chance that opportunities will emerge as the work progresses. The more people you and the students connect with, the more likely this becomes. Just be ready to shift plans when a great opportunity comes along.

While we should always aim for big ideas, don't be afraid to start projects on a smaller scale. A smaller challenge might put a time limit on the work in order to limit the scope or focus on a single subject or discipline; many challenges could be done in a week or a couple of months. Here are some examples of some smaller project ideas that could be done in weeks rather than months (note how they all start with active verbs):

- Plan an interactive, one-hour experience at a retirement home that will make the residents' day.
- Write, edit, and publish a book of poetry that will challenge people's visions of equality and justice. Sell the book and donate the funds to a local charity that you've researched.
- Fundraise, plan, and plant a garden made up of native plant species that will attract birds and butterflies.
- Research local historical figures and create an interactive display that will be shown at a local museum to generate community interest.
- Prepare a healthy menu of nonperishable food items for a low-income family and donate it to your local food bank.
- Challenge the school to a No Garbage Day by educating other classes, using social media, and running a competition. Measure and report the results of the amount of garbage produced on a regular day and the No Garbage Day.

Overcoming Obstacles

Planning this way can be a challenge. Here are some suggestions for how to respond to common issues.

It's difficult to envision how it all comes together. Some large chart paper and sticky notes can be a useful starting point as you begin to lay out the plan. Ask students and colleagues to provide additional input and ideas; don't feel obligated to do it all on your own. Constructing a challenge of this type is like putting together a large puzzle, so patience and open-mindedness are important.

As we discussed, for our environmental project, the three of us sat down with the overall curriculum expectations cut into strips on the table, looking for potential connections between different subject areas and brainstorming possible activities that students could be engaged in to learn them. This helped ensure that we were focused on the curriculum and maximizing opportunities to do cross-curricular work. It also forced us to think about the purpose of expectations in the curriculum: "Why is this in the curriculum, and what can be done with this skill or piece of knowledge to advance student work?"

It's difficult to work backward. Remember that you are really working backward *and* forward in the process. There's an ongoing negotiation among the challenge, student input, the curriculum, and any opportunities that arise along the way. Being flexible, as noted above, is important because the plan needs to change when opportunities or challenges present themselves. Remember that you don't have to carve out a path alone. If a new opportunity presents itself, or students come up with an idea that clearly needs to be incorporated into the work, invite them to think about how you might alter the direction of the work.

Taking It to the Next Level

As you become more comfortable with the idea of making meaning central to student work, here are some additional ideas about how to take the work up another notch.

Go long. Initially, it makes sense to start with smaller and more manageable challenges; you likely wouldn't want to start with a yearlong project like the one described in this chapter. Engaging students in work that takes a few days is a more manageable trial run. Then you can engage in long-term, multifaceted work where students' learning dramatically improves. The longer the work goes, the more likely it is that students will be able to have input and show leadership, building engagement while also making life easier for the teacher.

Invite students to help plan. Initially, you will want time to think in detail about what you want to accomplish, reflect on the curriculum pieces to integrate, and connect with potential partners about the work. As your confidence builds, however, there are opportunities to actively engage students from the beginning; this will be most likely to succeed where the students are old enough, and where they've had some experience with this work so that they know what the goal looks like (this is not advisable for a teacher and students with no experience of this kind).

You may be surprised to see what kind of ideas students will come up with when you present them with curricular expectations and ask how they can be connected to the project at hand. The teacher doesn't have to be source of all ideas and creativity in the classroom, and tapping into students' thoughts will make your job easier and give them a great sense of pride.

Invite others to participate on a bigger scale. As mentioned previously, our teamwork on the South Branch project allowed us to collaborate with, and even create some positive competition among, other classes and teachers. Doing a project of this magnitude without staff collaboration would have been incredibly difficult. Working with a bigger group can also make things more complicated because timelines and planning need to be synchronized. You may want to experiment in a limited way with this work to begin, but expanding the work outward to include others will ultimately allow you to become more ambitious and the learning to become more meaningful.

Go deeper using the limitless opportunities of the internet. With access to the internet, a class's reach can expand dramatically, not only in terms of research but also with the opportunity of engaging in meaningful work remotely. As an example, classes anywhere in the world can become microlenders (lending small amounts of money to economically disadvantaged people to help them to start a business or invest in equipment that will increase quality of life) using the website (www.kiva.org), evaluating the potential effectiveness of projects and changing lives on the other side of the world with their proceeds from fundraisers at home. Thanks to the internet, it's not necessary to embark on overseas trips to build global awareness and citizenship. Students aren't limited to thinking globally and acting locally; they can act globally, too.

Reflection

As you take the first steps toward making meaning central to student work, take stock of the following:

- What is the effect on your learning and motivation when you are given a task you see as important? What meaningful learning experiences have you had that you can share with students?
- How would you rate the meaning and importance of the level of work currently taking place in your classroom or school?
- What work are students currently doing that *they* would consider meaningful? What work would still be meaningful to them a month from now? A year from now?
- How lasting is the learning (i.e., is it short-term learning or something that students will use for the rest of their lives)?
- What kind of challenge could you issue to your students to drive their leadership and learning to the next level? What kind of opportunities exist in your local community that could form the basis of truly meaningful work?

Remember to think broadly about what resources are available in the community. What do you have that is walking distance from the school? The riverside park planned by South Branch, for example, was walking distance from the school, making it easy to get there, take photos and water samples, and map the area. Alternatively, think about the opportunities that technology can bring. Skype for Educators can allow teachers and classes to connect with other classes worldwide to explore a variety of areas of mutual interest. Better yet, combine the two by having students think globally and act locally.

Final Thoughts

In the end, our environmental project at South Branch was a resounding success. Despite their initial trepidation, our students did, in fact, reduce the environmental footprint of the school in measurable ways. Students also felt like they had had an impact on the community, inspiring community members and contributing directly to future community planning and land use. As a teacher, it was incredibly rewarding to see the students' confidence and sense of accomplishment.

When students are doing work that is meaningful to them, they will rise to the level of the expectations given to them. As a result, they will feel proud of the work they have done, and they will raise the level of expectations that they have for themselves going forward.

Teachers benefit almost as much as the students do from this. We all want our students to do well, push themselves, and be better than they thought they could be. There's a deep sense of personal pride in watching students produce work even they didn't realize they could produce. Another important benefit to the teacher? Assessment and evaluation become much, much easier, as we will discuss later in the book.

When students are passionate about what they are doing, learning happens naturally, and the work of the classroom becomes far easier for the teacher. One of the reasons teaching can be difficult at times is because so much of the work does not have direct and immediate meaning, requiring teachers to do everything they can to encourage, cajole, and sometimes pressure students into doing the work. When our project at South Branch was really clicking, the students would tell *me* what they were doing for the morning, and not the other way around—such was their organization, drive, and independence. Isn't this, fundamentally, what we want our students to learn? Shouldn't this be the fundamental goal of education?

A final benefit is that through students finding meaning in their work, teachers also find the meaning in theirs. Teachers whose classes are fired up about their learning are having fun, are more relaxed because they are not responsible for trying to drive all of the learning all of the time, and relish the ideas, creativity, and hard work of their students. When students are doing meaningful work, teachers are too.

So you've given students meaningful work. But what about the curriculum? How do we ensure that students are learning what they are supposed to? The next chapter explains how we can use curriculum as a resource for creating context and meaning and why meaningful student work and the curriculum don't have to be at odds with each other.

3

Contextualize the Curriculum

Step 2: Contextualize the Curriculum

The Big Ideas

- View the curriculum as a tool.
- Make the *why* explicit.
- Be flexible.

Activation Questions

Do you see the curriculum as a checklist or a toolbox?

How often do you refer to "covering" the curriculum?

When your students ask you, "Why are we learning this?" how satisfactory a response are you able to give them?

A colleague of mine, Principal Ewen McIntosh, described showing students in a grade 12 class the curriculum expectation they were studying as part of professional development classroom observation with teachers and administrators. One of the students interrupted the discussion, saying, "Wait a minute. Are you telling me that this is what we are doing? Everything we've done for the last 12 years is written down in those documents?" With months left in his high school education, this was the first time he'd ever seen the curriculum. When this was confirmed, he sat back in his chair and shook his head in amazement. "How come I've never seen this before?" he asked no one in particular. His question is a good one and deserving of an answer.

Most students' relationship with the curriculum is tenuous at best. Many know that it exists but have likely never looked at it. The question is, how can we use the curriculum to create more meaningful learning experiences?

View the Curriculum as a Tool

While curricula vary across regions, generally they are a list of skills and knowledge that have been deemed important enough to learn for students to become better thinkers and hopefully better citizens. Research shows that when students are able to apply new knowledge directly, particularly in hands-on activities, they are more likely to succeed in school (Bolak, Bialach, & Dunphy, 2005). It's equally important that it should be seen in an integrated fashion and not as a series of disjointed and artificially separated subject matter. Research says that an integrated approach to the curriculum "engages students, improves student learning, and increases student interest," which allows students to "link their experiences in the classroom to the real world and make sense of experiences from their lives" (Costley, 2015).

One thing that is important to remember is that knowledge is like potential energy: It doesn't do anything on its own, but it can be used to accomplish all sorts of interesting things. Herein lies part of the new relationship with knowledge. Learning about global warming is not about the rote memorization of the amount of CO^2 required to shift global temperatures a degree. It's about helping us reevaluate our relationship with the planet, economics, politics, ecology, sustainability, the media, and how we live our daily lives, but ultimately it's about what we can and will do individually and collectively to mitigate the effects of climate change and make sweeping changes moving forward. It's about action. Knowledge needs context. Knowledge needs to be used.

Part of the role of the teacher is to encourage students, as learners, to become *users* of knowledge and not simply possessors of it. When knowledge has purpose, it has relevance. Students pursuing projects of interest suddenly become seekers and users of knowledge. They understand the importance of knowledge and develop an active relationship with it.

Looking at the curriculum as a tool for doing something *with* fundamentally changes our relationship with it. By prioritizing the purpose of the curriculum over rote knowledge, we put its usefulness ahead of its potential randomness as a checklist to be worked through. We put the curriculum second.

Where Do I Begin?

In this new pedagogy, we want to look at the curriculum as a toolbox of skills and knowledge that serve a variety of purposes. Here are some places to begin.

Put the curriculum second to a great idea when planning a project. One source of debate when planning real-world projects is whether the curriculum or idea comes first in your planning. In my experience, it is easier to come up with a good idea and then look for ways to integrate the curriculum into it, rather than the other way around.

The reason for this is that curricula tend to be wide-ranging and in most cases quite long. They are also of the educational world rather than the real world. While they contain skills and knowledge that you can do something with, they are not typically explicitly laid out to make this easy. If you start with a list of curriculum expectations and try to dream up something that students can do with them, then you often will end up with something convoluted and artificial in nature, ultimately ending up with something of an unfortunate, forced mess.

When you start with a great idea, you can often weave curriculum expectations into the idea by using the knowledge or skill in a more meaningful way. It is transformed into applied knowledge and practiced with purpose. You may not integrate dozens of expectations, but the ones that you do integrate (ideally, ones you have prioritized) will genuinely be learned by the students because they will be doing something purposeful with the knowledge. For example, if the curriculum says students need to write persuasively, we can ask students to write a persuasive letter about changing a classroom rule, which is sure to prompt some debate. Many students will be able to come up with some good arguments, but others are likely to make a lackluster effort because it may not be all that important to them. However, if we ask students to complete a grant application to raise funds to support important work they are doing, the amount of student buy-in will rise dramatically because there are real potential benefits to the work, as well as an audience outside the school to impress with their reasoning. Note that in the second example the curriculum is supporting the student work, rather than acting as an end of its own. That is, *we need to raise money to support our project, and we can use the curricular expectation around persuasive writing to help us do so.*

While you want to start with a great idea first and integrate the curriculum second, there is often back-and-forth with that approach. You might, for example, have curriculum expectations you would really like to integrate, and there might be easy ways to change the project idea to accommodate them. This is part of the back-and-forth negotiation described in the last chapter.

When delivering professional development to teachers and administrators on this kind of work, I'm often asked, "This all sounds great, but how can I find the time to actually do this kind of work with my students? As it is, I have a hard enough time getting through the curriculum." My response is to point out that the tendency to view the curriculum as a checklist creates the time crunch in our classrooms because expectations are tackled individually, rather than organizing the learning around several complementary expectations simultaneously. In response, I'll often ask, "If we work today to create a real-world learning experience that will allow you to evaluate seven or eight curricular expectations, how much time could you then reasonably devote to it?" The answer, of course, is that you can spend a lot of time on an experience like this, and by doing so you can slow the pace of the classroom and go much deeper into the learning. This, I'll point out, is good for both students and teachers.

Integrate the curriculum. The artificial separation of the curriculum into distinct subjects or strands is problematic because it sends the incorrect message to students that the knowledge is not connected. This disjointed view of the world is particularly problematic when so many of the issues we face collectively, as well as individually, require a multidisciplinary approach. It's also a uniquely academic construct and not a reflection of the real world.

If you work, for example, as a web designer, you will be expected to communicate and consult with a client (oral and written communication), understand the goals that they're trying to achieve (business), develop a sense of what message they want to send to potential customers (marketing), work as part of a team to meet the customer's needs (collaborative skills), write up a persuasive proposal (English), make decisions about color and design (visual art), and have the technical know-how to make it all come off (computer studies). It's not enough to understand the programming language. As another example, think about the wide range of skills and knowledge that you require as an educator. They likely include expertise in pedagogy (education), under-standing of child development (psychology), computer skills (technology), and creating a healthy classroom environment (sociology), not to mention subject matter knowledge. There's also a good chance that you have some expertise in political skills, which allows you to work effectively with students, parents, colleagues, and administration. It's never just about one thing.

A useful practice when trying to integrate multiple subject areas can be to physically lay out the overall expectations that you have for your class or course and look to see if you can find some natural patterns in them (e.g., photocopy them, cut them into individual expectations, then work with a colleague to group them around project components). The groupings that you come up with might, in return, inspire ideas about possible projects. The goal then becomes to work back and forth between the curriculum and project idea brainstorming, where a project idea might allow you to see another con-nection to curriculum that you hadn't seen as initially connected. The early planning stages thus become a sort of negotiation between the curriculum and your best ideas. This is how we were able to combine expectations from language arts, science, math, geography, visual art, technology, health, and even some history in the South Branch project.

A final note: If we see curricula as tools, thus collectively making them an educational toolbox, separating the subjects out into distinct pieces and asking students only to use one at a time is a little like asking a plumber to fix a problem with only a single wrench. Students should be free to use whichever tools are required to get the job done.

Don't play. Do. In the spirit of trying to give the curriculum context, teachers will sometimes have students engage in simulations to help them see the purpose of the learning. While this is often a good way to generate interest, and more desirable than a traditional lecture format, it is even better if you can bring the learning to the world outside the classroom. Figure 3.1 includes some examples.

Moving from a simulation to a real-world context brings students lessons that they would not otherwise get. All the ideas in the right-hand column, for example, require that students interact, organize, collaborate, compro-mise, persuade, and take action, none of which takes place in the traditional approach. A simulation is a great place to start (and could be used as a step-ping-stone toward even more meaningful work), but whenever possible, push the learning experience to the next level.

FIGURE 3.1		
Moving Learning to the Real World		
Traditional Model	**Simulation**	**Real World**
Read about democracy and the electoral process and take a test.	Hold a mock election.	Become involved in local politics by attending a meeting and lobbying for change.
Learn about ecology from a science textbook.	Create a poster showing a design for a renewable community.	Partner with the community to clean up an unused green space and plant native flowers to attract birds and insects.
Read a magazine article about human migration.	Host a forum to discuss issues facing refugees.	Organize a community fundraiser to support groups helping refugees settle in your local community.

Aim for students to comprehend, not cover, the curriculum. One of my pet peeves as a principal is when educators discuss the importance of "covering the curriculum." In a good-natured way, I officially banned the phrase from all staff meetings. While it appears to be a reasonable statement, the implication is that the curriculum is something to be gone over rather than learned. If the curriculum is treated as a checklist of subjects that should be covered, then what you end up with is a wide range of disconnected facts and ideas spoken about while students are in the room. Learning is not about covering. It's about *uncovering* a range of skills and knowledge and using them in purposeful ways so that we will remember them, use them again, and get better at them through practice.

As a former English teacher, I recall stating, with some frustration and knowing irony, that I couldn't understand how my 12th graders couldn't write an English essay when I had taught these skills to the same students in grade 9. It was interesting that after being taught by me, and having the skills reinforced by two colleagues in the intervening years, they didn't have the skills three years later. This is one of the first times that I really started to reflect on the gap between teaching and learning: the assumption that the teacher (an external factor) can cause learning (an internal process) to take place within a student. This fundamental misconception has led to countless frustrations for both students and teachers. Students don't understand what they are supposed to know; teachers can't understand why students don't know it when they "taught it to them."

To help close this gap, ask yourself the following question: At the end of the process, do the students now possess the knowledge or skill that you think you taught them? In other words, if you change the context or come back to the skill or knowledge later, do they still have it, or was it simply stored in short-term memory to complete a task or test?

Interestingly, the classroom is probably the only context where teaching and learning takes place in such a restrictive context. For instance, a basketball coach would never use a similar model:

1. Basketball coach talks to students about what a jump shot, layup, and defensive stance look like.
2. Students take a test to show whether they know what is involved in a jump shot, layup, and defensive stance.
3. Coach grades the test and takes the 12 highest grades to make the team's roster.

The process obviously looks ridiculous in this context, so why is it any less ridiculous in the classroom? Deep learning takes place in a meaningful context with a specific goal in mind, and that goal is not to pass the test.

Think like a coach. As an example of what the first steps toward teaching *should* look like, let's spend a little more time on the coaching analogy. If we replace the process outlined above with one that is more appropriate, what we find is a process that is more student-based, more reactive, more focused, and indeed more complex:

1. Players and coach start with a common, clearly understood goal: to compete in and win basketball games.
2. The coach evaluates players by taking them through a series of drills focused on a wide range of skills and knowledge.
3. The coach prioritizes the skills that are most important to the players' future success in a basketball game. The practices are built around the fundamentals before moving on to more complex ideas.
4. The skills themselves are further broken down into components. This allows this coach to see, for example, why a player is having a hard time doing a layup. Is it coordinating his steps? Is it the body position? Is it the way she is using her hands? Players are thus given drills in increasingly smaller groups to help them learn the skill. Progressing on to the next

skill is dependent on the player learning the skill and not on a schedule that the coach has predetermined.

5. Players work their way up to scrimmages and then games, returning frequently to practice, where the coach takes what is learned about the players through observation of them in a game situation to determine what they need next on the continuum of skills.

It's interesting to see how much more student-based this process is than a traditional classroom approach, as well as the extent to which it is dependent on players demonstrating their learning. A basketball coach doesn't say to a player that continues to struggle with a layup, "We've already covered that; it's too late. You failed layups. Now we're working on jump shots."

Note that the coach, like a teacher, is still vitally important to the success of the players. When we talk about the changing role of teachers, some people begin to fear that they will be sidelined and somehow their importance will be diminished. On the contrary: a wide range of skills, knowledge, observation and reflection are crucial to being a good coach. Effective coaches are engaged and focused on student learning. They are highly skilled teachers.

Help students build a relationship with the curriculum. One element of schooling that remains curious is how frequently students' relationship with the curriculum is often extremely limited. It is, perhaps, a reflection of the traditional model of schooling where the teacher is the fount of all knowledge and the curriculum is a mystery. Clearly, things have begun to change in recent years, but why the continued reticence to include the curriculum in direct discussion with students?

There are likely a number of reasons, including past practice (it's just not often done) and that the language can be difficult to understand for younger students. However, there is another reason that may also explain part of the reticence: Teachers are not teaching the curriculum all of the time. It can be very easy to be sidelined into planning activities rather than ensuring students are learning the curriculum. That's not to say that the curriculum, or at least elements of it, may not be present in the lesson or activity, but it can sometimes be an afterthought. Focusing students and their parents on the curriculum documents can feel a little like showing them the operating manual, but understanding the purpose of what students are doing and building relevance into their learning are important first steps toward creating a more meaningful educational experience.

Overcoming Obstacles

Here are some ways to respond to challenges that might emerge.

The administrator or board wants teachers to treat the curriculum like a checklist. Using the curriculum as a tool is not incompatible with being accountable for having students learn the curriculum. In fact, in some ways it might be easier. When students are actively engaged in learning, the teacher has more flexibility to meaningfully track student learning and provide more detailed feedback.

The curriculum feels disconnected and somewhat random. Not all curricula are well designed for putting the learning into context. That said, none of them are purely random; there are always patterns and purpose. Digging below the surface of why specific knowledge and skills are on the curriculum is important and something we discuss in the next strategy.

Make the *Why* Explicit

One of the most common questions at school with the least satisfying answers is "Why are we learning this?" The question, on its face, is entirely reasonable. Understanding *why* one is doing something is central to establishing a context and purpose for the learning and is a basic human need.

With apologies, because we all likely recognize something we've said before in this list, these are the worst answers to the question "Why are we learning this?"

"Because it's in the curriculum."

As we've discussed, most students have no idea what the curriculum is. The answer also places the rationale for learning far outside the classroom. A much more satisfying answer to the question would provide more immediate context and relevancy. Consider this response: "The curriculum requires that we learn how to manage data. In our case, we are going to collect data as part of our plan to start a classroom business, and the information we gather from other students will inform our marketing plan, help us to make decisions, and increase the likelihood of our success."

This response still references the curriculum, but it's easy to see how the addition of context and relevancy makes it much more likely that students will both accept and understand the purpose of the learning.

"Because it's on the test next Wednesday."

This answer is worse than the first one. Now the decontextualized learning is being evaluated in a format that exists in almost no other context than school. In this case, the completion of the test itself is the purpose and not the learning. Consider this alternative: "The curriculum requires that we learn to write effectively in a variety of formats. We're going to use this skill when we write biographies of soldiers from the local community who made the ultimate sacrifice, in our partnership with our area's history museum. I will be holding writing conferences with you regularly over the next few weeks to help you improve your ability to demonstrate this expectation and assessing your work this way."

"Because if you go on to study biochemical engineering, in your third year of university this will be really important."

This response attempts to establish relevancy by suggesting a specific context in the future (ironically, in another educational setting) wherein the information will be important. However, it won't be relevant for most students' futures. As teachers, we need to be prepared to answer the question of why we are doing something in the here and now and not in some mythical point in the future. A better answer might be the following: "Our work to build a community garden requires us to understand concepts around area and volume, as well as various forms of measurement; these are also in our math curriculum. With spring quickly approaching, we will apply our math learning to our work in the community shortly."

"Why are we learning this?" is an important question and not one that should be taken lightly. As learners, students deserve to know the answer to the question. So, how do we do this? By going back to the curriculum and asking ourselves one simple question: Why is this in the curriculum?

There are countless curricula out there of varying length, focus, and quality, but all of them have some essential elements in common, and therein lies the starting point for making them meaningful:

- **Curricula provide a list of knowledge and skills that students should know and do.** Some curricula focus more on knowledge while others bring more of a balance with skills, but fundamentally they provide a list of things students should be able to know or do.

- **Curricula are constructed purposefully.** They are not intended to be a random sampling of skills and ideas but rather a vetted list of skills and knowledge deemed to be important. In most instances, problems with curricula are based on prioritization. The debate is not over what is important but rather what is *most* important.

- **Creating context for the curriculum is derived from answering the question "Why is this in the curriculum?"** While this seems rather simple, on some level, one of the primary reasons that many schools struggle to make their relevance clear is because this important question is forgotten. The curriculum, in many ways, is not as important as the purpose behind it.

For example, if the curriculum says that 8th graders will "generate, gather, and organize ideas and information to write for an intended purpose and audience" (Ontario Ministry of Education, 2006), the answers to the question "Why is this on the curriculum?" could be many, but fundamentally, writing is about the ability to communicate with purpose to a specific audience. This expectation is not on the curriculum because it was deemed important that students write a five-paragraph essay on *To Kill a Mockingbird* for which they receive a grade. In fact, most curricula don't say anything like this; the actual interpretation of what it should look like is left up to the teacher who, logically, is often inclined to teach the way they were taught. However, the purpose and audience intended in writing is not always the teacher; in fact, in the future, it won't be for a teacher at all and certainly won't take place in the very specific context of the classroom. We want students to be able to communicate with the world around them in a meaningful way and to recognize that different audiences require different approaches. That's not to say that students shouldn't learn how to write a five-paragraph essay, but if the education system is struggling with relevance, this is surely not the way to create it. If students are being asked to write a newspaper article, then the article should be informative, interesting, and printed in a newspaper, whether it's a school newspaper (good) or a small local paper that will accept submissions (better). If students are writing a persuasive letter, it should be written about an issue that they really feel strongly about to someone who can do something about the issue because that's why we write persuasive letters.

Where Do I Begin?

Redefining our students' relationship with the curriculum starts with redefining our own relationship with it. We need to remember to treat the curriculum not as the last word on learning but as a starting point for our own skilled interpretation about why that skill or knowledge has been included in the curriculum and our ideas about how to create learning experiences where students can use it purposefully.

Have a concrete answer to the "Why?" question. Whenever you are looking at a curriculum expectation, ask, "Why is this on the curriculum?" and try to find ways to have students use the skill or knowledge for its intended purpose. In many cases, the problem is not with the curriculum itself but with how we use it. The curriculum is not a legal text that we read and adhere to with explicit precision. It is a jumping-off point for creating learning experiences. Having clarity when students ask this question will also help drive student learning.

Returning briefly to the environmental project at South Branch from Chapter 2, Figure 3.2 gives examples of some of the curriculum expectations that students learned over the course of the year and the answers we gave for why they needed to learn them (these expectations are taken from the Ontario curriculum).

FIGURE 3.2	
Why Do We Have to Learn This?	
Curriculum Expectation	**Why Do We Have to Learn This?**
Communicate orally in a clear, coherent manner, using a structure and style appropriate to both the topic and the intended audience.	Because we are going to run assemblies for the entire school, and it's important that we are able to communicate clearly.
Assess the impacts of human activities and technologies on the environment, and evaluate ways of controlling these impacts.	Because in order to reduce the ecological footprint of the school, you need to understand how ecosystems work and the impact that humans have on them.
Write complex texts of different lengths using a wide range of forms.	Because we are publishing newspaper articles in the local paper to persuade people to reduce their environmental footprint at home, and they won't take us seriously if we aren't able to represent ourselves well in text and communicate clearly.

Curriculum Expectation	Why Do We Have to Learn This?
Determine, through investigation, the relationships among fractions, decimals, percentages, and ratios.	Because we are using this knowledge to build properly scaled models of our park redevelopment plan, which will be on display at City Hall, shared with the mayor and council, and photographed by the media, and if they are not built to scale, then it will detract from the overall message we are trying to convey.

There are a couple of things worth noting about this list. First, we answered the question by asking ourselves what the purpose of the skill or knowledge was for. Second, in each case the curriculum was being actively used for a specific purpose that had meaning outside the classroom. Students were evaluated individually, but the primary purpose of learning the curriculum expectation was not "Because I have to evaluate you on this" but because the task required it.

There were some expectations that simply didn't fit into the broader project, and they generally were managed in a more traditional way. It's likely not possible to connect everything because in most cases the curricula were not designed to be used in such an integrated way. However, most expectations did connect in some way; interestingly, the ones that didn't felt somewhat artificial by contrast.

Share the curriculum with the students. It's important to recognize that the curriculum is the basis for what we do in the class and thus is an important meaning maker. Not sharing the curriculum with students is akin to your district sending out directives about what you should be doing in your classroom without sharing a strategic plan or the broader goals.

Let students see what you are doing. Remember, the document is the center of what you are doing *collectively*; it's just as important to them as it is to you. You will likely need to provide some explanation, or even alternative wording, for younger students to understand what's expected. This is entirely reasonable because *interpreter of the curriculum* is a key part of your job.

When it's developmentally appropriate, discuss with your students how they would like to demonstrate some of the curriculum expectations. In other words, negotiate the curriculum. There are countless ways that the knowledge and skills can be demonstrated. If students have input into how the learning will be shown, you increase their drive by increasing their autonomy, mastery, and purpose, as Daniel Pink urges. It's also likely that students will dream up some great ideas about how their learning can be demonstrated. Part of what makes change in the classroom so challenging is that in the traditional model, the teacher is expected to come up with all the ideas. That's a tremendous burden and frankly not all that fair. You have a room full of people to work with; see your students as a resource. What better way to teach students the value of collaboration than by negotiating what we do in class and how we do it and by showing them how their ideas have made your ideas better.

As part of a project I was involved in, we brought groups of students and their teachers together to do some planning. Students had to come up with an innovative program idea and put a plan together to implement it in collaboration with their teacher. We said to the students, "Your teachers will need to evaluate your work, so here is a link to the curriculum documents. Take some time to go through them and find some connections that you can make with your project that will allow your teacher to evaluate your work and write a report card comment." The students quickly found connections and, in some cases, made slight changes to their plans in order to connect more curricular expectations. For example, by adding a presentation to the work they were doing, they recognized that it would allow their teacher to evaluate their oral communication skills. It made life easier for the teachers, while also allowing students to answer for themselves the question "Why do we have to learn this?"

Remember the importance of context in learning. All learning has to take place within the context of something we currently know. When developing ideas with students, remember to ensure that they have some potential connection to a context they already understand. For example, a conversation about starting a small business might begin with jobs they have done in the past, small businesses that they currently frequent, and friends and neighbors who are in business. Students can understand complex ideas, but they have to start their development of these concepts from a familiar context.

Help students understand the importance of metacognition. Research has shown that *metacognition*—the conscious understanding of how we learn—has a strong correlation with academic performance. Research on metacognition states that students need to "be aware of their learning, to evaluate their learning needs, to generate strategies to meet their needs, and to implement those strategies" (Hacker, Dunlosky, & Graesser, 2009). In other words, students need to understand both *why* they are learning what they are learning and *how* they are learning it.

In younger grades, it may be necessary to reword or rework expectations so that students can understand them. Having said that, it is still important that they are exposed to the language used in curricula, because reading a curriculum is like reading any other technical document. It has a specific form, uses certain diction, and provides clarification in very particular ways. Talking about these qualities with students is an important first step in learning and shouldn't be seen as a waste of time.

Recognize that the majority of curricula do not say "as evaluated in the form of a written test." Sometimes written tests are an appropriate way to demonstrate learning, but there are plenty of other ways to do it that are fairer to the students in the class who aren't great writers or who don't work well in timed, high-pressure situations. In the real world, we tend to be evaluated on how we *do* something, not on how well we write about something we might do (e.g., we don't take a test when it comes time to be evaluated on our teaching; we are observed teaching). Following these suggestions will also allow you to make your evaluation of student work more meaningful and more performance-based. Fortunately, it also tends to reduce the amount of time you spend at night grading a big pile of tests because students will spend their time demonstrating their learning and their use of the learning rather than simply writing about it. We'll dig further into evaluation later in the book.

Overcoming Obstacles

Here's a thought about how to manage an obstacle related to explaining expectations.

It's not clear to teachers why this expectation is on the curriculum. It's probably time to consult with your colleagues. If you don't know why something is important, it's going to be impossible to communicate to your students why they need to learn it. It's also problematic on a professional level because we, as educators, have to see the purpose in our work to derive satisfaction. Nothing will drain motivation faster than feeling there's no real meaning behind the work.

Another strategy is to check expectations for both the previous grade and the next grade up. Curricula are often written in a way that builds from year to year, so looking at the expectation in a broader context can help us to see where the learning is coming from and where it is going.

Be Flexible

We've already discussed the need to be flexible in our approach to planning. Here are a few strategies that can help us to get started.

Where Do I Begin?

Here are some additional thoughts about how to make better use of the curriculum.

View curricular expectations as a hierarchy. Again, not all curriculum expectations are created equally. Some are far more important in terms of both what students can do with them and the foundational role that they play in learning going forward. Treating the curriculum expectations as a homogeneous checklist deprives students the lesson of learning the difference between what is important and what is simply interesting. To take the earlier basketball metaphor a little further, a student has to be able to dribble down the court and pass the ball before she or he learns a fadeaway jump shot or how to set a pick. There are need-to-haves and nice-to-haves, and being able to distinguish between the two is important.

This is an area where teachers have an important role to play. As experts on the curriculum, we can help students to understand that not all meaning and skills are created equally. We can teach them important lessons about prioritization and foundational knowledge. This can also help students recognize the gaps in their own learning and understand that sometimes we need to cycle back to an earlier concept if we are going to have success going forward. Students who haven't learned their times tables, for example, are going to have a more difficult time figuring out equivalent fractions and may need to cycle back to that earlier knowledge to move forward.

Recognize that it won't all fit. Because most curricula are not designed specifically for supporting learning of this nature, it's very likely that you will have pieces that simply won't fit into your real-world projects. Don't force it: Pushing curriculum expectations into the project in an artificial way tends to undermine the legitimacy of the other work you are doing.

Have a discussion with students about curriculum that doesn't really fit into their project work but is still important in other contexts. In my experience, they will understand that sometimes it may be necessary to do some more traditional-style school work.

The good news is that there are signs in other parts of the world of curricula being shifted to make this problem a thing of the past. Finland is moving toward organizing learning around what they call *phenomenon*, topic-based teaching where all students are involved in learning about issues from a multidisciplinary perspective at least once a day. A study about the European Union, for example, would include work on economics, history, geography, and language studies (Garner, 2015).

Until most jurisdictions adopt this integrated curriculum approach, this will continue to be a problem. Because most curricula are not designed for integration from day one, there will always be parts that won't fit. Students will understand when you say, "We need to take a break from our project work tomorrow to learn some curriculum that is not tied to your current work." After all, it's what most of them have been experiencing for most of their educational career. Keeping it separate communicates that this is a bit of traditional schooling that is required and will avoid undermining the meaning of the other work they are doing.

Overcoming Obstacles

Here is a suggestion for managing a highly prescriptive curriculum.

The curriculum is highly specific and heavy on knowledge. If you have a curriculum that is heavily structured and focused on specific knowledge, it's important to take a step back from it and look for the overall rationale and big ideas that lie behind it. Being flexible with the curriculum means that sometimes we are looking at honoring the spirit of the curriculum as much as we are looking at it for specific learning goals. It comes back to the question "Why is this on the curriculum?" There is a reason it's been structured that way, and by taking a bird's-eye view of it, we can see more clearly the intentionality in it.

Taking It to the Next Level

As you become more comfortable with contextualizing the curriculum, here are some additional ideas about how to make the work even more sophisticated.

Involve students in curriculum interpretation. While this may not work for very young students, giving students expectations and teaching them how to do a close textual analysis of the expectation can be a great way to emphasize the collaborative nature of your work with them. This may be a real challenge at first but will become easier with practice.

Consider this list of powerful questions as a starting point:

1. Here is a curricular expectation that we need to learn this year. What do you think this means?

2. How could we use this skill or knowledge in a purposeful way?

3. How do you think you could demonstrate to me that you know and understand this (knowledge) or are able to do this (skill)?

A classroom engaged in this sort of metacognitive work is one where the teacher will infrequently need to answer the question "Why are we learning this?" because students were involved in formulating the response to the question from the beginning.

Involve students in the planning. Once you have become more comfortable with the process of planning with a wide range of curricular expectations from different subject areas, why not involve students themselves? There's a good chance that they will see connections that you won't, and they may even find it easier to see how to make the learning relevant because they will automatically consider the expectations from their point of view and context. This strategy requires a certain amount of experience and confidence because discussions this open-ended could lead in all sorts of unexpected directions.

Reflection

Here are some questions to reflect on while you consider how to renegotiate your students' relationship with the curriculum:

- Do your students know that there is a curriculum that underpins the work you do together, and have they seen it?
- Do they know and understand the curriculum expectations?
- Can they answer the question "Why are we learning this?" Can you?
- Do they have a specific purpose for what they are learning?
- Are they being asked to apply the knowledge and skills from the curriculum in a meaningful way?
- Do your students see the knowledge and skills they are learning from the curriculum as purposeful and relevant to their lives *today?*
- Do they see them as tools being added to their intellectual toolbox?
- In your practice, do you flexibly work back and forth between the curriculum, meaningful student work, and learning opportunities that present themselves to you throughout the year?

- Are your students clear about how they are evaluated in relation to the curriculum, and do they receive regular feedback about how they are performing?

Final Thoughts

The curriculum is often treated as a limitation. It's time to change the way we think and act and to reevaluate how much of a limitation this really is. The notion of covering the curriculum—that is, going through it like a check-list—has no bearing on real-world learning and making that learning useful. It focuses too much on teaching and not enough on learning.

Similarly, treating subject areas like they are truly distinct from each other, rather than an arbitrary organizational structure, denies students the important learning about how knowledge, and the world itself, is deeply inter-connected. We live in a complex, interconnected world that requires complex, interconnected solutions to its problems.

Create Space to Learn

Step 3: Create Space to Learn

The Big Ideas

- Make room for active learners.

- Create space to fail.

- Change the environment to change the learner.

- Resource student work appropriately.

- Model lifelong learning.

Activation Questions

How much of your school day is driven by student interest and initiative?

To what extent do you use choice, and accept student suggestions, as a part of your teaching practice?

How are you honoring the learning that students are doing outside school in the classroom?

What are you doing to ensure that students can see themselves reflected in your classroom?

We ordered our first 3D printer at the school. It functions a little like a regular printer, but instead of printing ink it melts a colored filament (which looks like fishing line) into shapes that you have designed on the computer. As the head of the printer shifts back and forth, what you created in a design program begins to appear, like magic, inside the box of the printer.

When the printer arrived in October, I gave it to a teacher named Chad Norbraten who was teaching computers, business, and math. Handing him the box, I joked, "Here's a 3D printer. Do something interesting with it." Chad, being the bright guy that he is, brought it to a business technology class and gave it to small group of students and said to them, "Here's a 3D printer. Do something interesting with it."

The students took the printer out of the box and set it up. None of the staff in the school knew how to use it, including Chad and me, so it was up to them to figure it out. The students promptly printed out a figure whose plan came with the printer, and within a few days began to print off other plans they had found on the internet. They downloaded different types of design software and quickly learned how to modify the designs they were finding, learning the limitations and possibilities of the machine and sharing their learning with classmates and their teacher.

A group of students, led by Nick and Austin, decided that as part of their class project–which involved setting up a small business, including building an e-commerce site and marketing a product–they would build a business that made customized phone cases. The idea was that by putting the school's initials right into the cases, highlighting specialized programs (like the school's popular CrossFit exercise program), and being able to print in different colors, they could make a case that could compete on the market.

It was at this point that Kyle joined the group. Kyle had a spare study period at the same time as the class; he was so interested in what they were doing, he began to attend the class and skip his spare, such was the level of engagement that was taking place. In short order the group accomplished the following things:

- They set up a website to sell their products. We received permission from the board to set up a functioning e-commerce site, which was the first time this had had happened.

- Using Skype, they connected with a start-up executive in the United Kingdom whose company also built 3D phone cases. He gave them feedback on their designs and told them they could adapt the company's designs and sell them as long as the money was returned to the school.

- They came to our parent council meeting to show off the technology, which resulted in the school getting another printer donated by impressed parents.

- The students visited a staff meeting to show other staff how the technology worked and what it could do.

- Visiting grade 7 and 8 classes, as well as an after-school high school credit that 8th graders could take, they began to train younger students on how to use the technology.

- They successfully made a pitch to the board's head of information technology, who agreed to give the school an additional $5,000 to support the program.

- They connected with freelance programmers on the other side of the world and explored the possibility of subcontracting out some of their work (they didn't end up doing this, but what an interesting conundrum it would have created. Do we deduct grades for cheating or praise them for their ingenuity and acting like a real business?).

- They went to a business competition and took home first prize.

Over the course of approximately eight months, the students went from never having seen the technology before to starting a small business, training more than a hundred students and teachers on the technology, raising more than $7,000 for the school, and becoming experts in 3D printing. Beyond that, they led us to reflect on the educational paradigm of the school when we ran a course to meet their needs.

Make Room for Active Learners

In order for learning to be truly effective, there needs to be room for the learner's previous experiences, interests, passions, and ideas. Highly regimented, teacher-driven classrooms do not permit this space and thus have limited effectiveness as learning environments. Learning is an activity. It involves action, thought, questioning, experimenting, challenging, and refining as the learners work their way toward understanding a new concept. Classrooms where the teacher talks most of the time while students sit quietly do not recognize learning as an activity.

It's worth returning to Daniel Pink's work here. In order to create drive, we need autonomy, mastery, and purpose. If we don't create space, we can get compliance or defiance, but little else. We enter a state of deep learning when we find the work interesting and relevant and we can see ourselves in the work.

Thus, part of bringing education to the next stage is creating space in the learning environment *for* the learner. While this seems rather obvious, many students find very little of themselves in a traditional class. This is also creating an increasingly awkward gap between the passive experience they have in school and the active and passionate learning experiences they are having outside school where, with a little curiosity and motivation, there is very little they can't learn to do.

We have entered an age where being an active learner has never been easier. You can learn to do almost anything via the internet. For example, an 8th grader at my school, Jordan, was intrigued by a discussion about hovercrafts in class and discovered how to make one on YouTube. A few days later, the entire class was on a basketball court getting rides on his hovercraft, powered by a gas-fueled leaf blower. Of course, there are thousands of students like Jordan experimenting with all sorts of learning inspired by the internet; while some might dismiss this as curiosity and play, it is also indicative of a dramatic shift in learning that requires an equally dramatic shift in education.

Traditional educators may bemoan the current lack of student attention, the distraction of electronics in the classroom, and students' inability to sit quietly and take notes. The fact is that passive learning has never been the best way to learn, and thanks to technology, the current generation is actively rejecting it. You can imagine, for example, the project that Jordan engaged in as part of a university engineering program 20 years ago. Students would have learned about friction, air pressure, displacement, and so on before trying to assemble their own hovercraft. Jordan already has a much better understanding of these concepts than he would have gained from listening to a lecture, and more important, he is planning additional improvements to the design, doing further research, and learning to innovate. This is the basis for deep, lasting learning.

Where Do I Begin?

Creating space for student learning means entering into a learning dialogue with your students and consciously leaving space in your plans so they can bring themselves to the learning. Here are a few steps you can use to get started.

Reexamine some of your current lessons, assignments, or projects and think about how you could change them to create more learning

space for students. If the work currently gives them no options, then build options into it. If it has some options, brainstorm with the class to come up with even more. When they come up with something, find a way to say yes. Part of our job is to direct students as required but also to be open-minded to the ways they might want to learn. We need to work from a position of trust, and if the plan doesn't work out, there's a good chance that the students might learn more anyway. So-called failure is a learning opportunity.

Integrate a genius hour into your classroom routine. Genius hour (sometimes called 20 percent time, FedEx time, or Google time) is a strategy that we've used to great success at my own school, and it has become increasingly popular in schools across North America. The idea is to emulate private companies that have started to provide employees time to drive their own learning by giving them paid time to explore side projects. In the case of Google, the practice famously led to popular applications like Gmail.

In school, genius hour involves setting aside time on a weekly basis when students determine their own learning. The teacher typically provides some sort of planner to help students organize themselves and then works to support their learning. We have seen students make a horse blanket from recycled materials, make a prom dress from duct tape, create a video game, write a scratch-and-sniff cookbook of Italian recipes (they smelled of rosemary, oregano, etc., depending on what the recipe called for), start to write their first novel, and smelt aluminum (at home with adult supervision, of course). It offers a fascinating look into the interests and learning passions of the students.

Create time in class to discuss with students what they are learning outside class. Commit to a weekly shared learning time and help students understand the value of their learning outside school. Sharing your own learning from outside school with students can also reinforce its importance and let them know that you are also a lifelong learner.

Maintain a learning wall (real or virtual) where you share the broad range of learning that the students are doing. You can then use those ideas to create new, relevant learning experiences for the students. For example, if you have a group of Minecraft enthusiasts, you could have them lead their classmates through a lesson on how to use the software to set up biomes as part of your science studies or rebuild a famous building or battlefield in history.

Ask students what their learning goals are at the beginning of the year. In a traditional classroom, *we* provide students an overview of everything they are going to learn in our class for the year on the first day of school.

This sends a clear message that we are in control of the learning and that students will have little say. Think about how the message is changed when we ask them what their goals are for the year. When a colleague of mine, Heather Mortimer, did this with one of her senior English classes with a number of struggling learners, they were very open about the fact that they wanted to become better writers and were self-conscious about how they looked on paper. This was an extremely useful piece of information for her: The students had a very specific and relevant goal to focus on with a clear curricular connection.

Overcoming Obstacles

Creating space for learning is a change for both the teacher and the students. Here are possible responses to some of the challenges you might run into.

Students are not using the space teachers have given them productively. It is possible to create too much space for students. Students need some definition around their work. You will know if there is too much space because students will have a hard time getting started. They won't know which general direction they should be headed in and will likely show signs of frustration. The space still needs to be defined. Some teachers, for example, try a genius hour without success; this is almost never due to a lack of ideas by the students but rather a lack of structure, process, and feedback from the teacher. In experimenting with the concept of creating more space, it makes sense to open it up gradually by, for example, removing certain parameters from projects you might have assigned in the past.

Providing a specific goal, without telling students how to achieve it (as discussed in Chapter 2), is one good way to create focus while still leaving lots of space for students to shape the learning. Where teachers tend to get into trouble is when there are so few guidelines that students have no idea where to even begin.

Students are having a hard time getting started. Building from the last point, it's the unfortunate case that some students have a hard time generating ideas. In most cases, this probably wasn't an issue for them in kindergarten (kindergarten students are rarely at a loss for what to do), but creativity can be like a muscle that is infrequently exercised. Spending time brainstorming with students, asking them about interests outside school, and pooling ideas from other students to share on an idea board can be good ways to scaffold the initial process and help them get out of the starter blocks.

Classmates are often the best resource if students are struggling to come up with an idea.

My administrator or colleagues think I'm wasting time or am giving students too much say. It's important to communicate with others as we embark on new strategies. Not everyone is going to be comfortable with the idea of creating more space for students, in part because it means giving up some of the power in the classroom. Spending time explaining to other professionals the rationale for doing things differently, inviting them into the classroom to see how these ideas can work, and having them talk to the students about their own educational experiences can lead to productive dialogue.

Create Space to Fail

Research out of the National Institute of Education in Singapore reinforces the importance of failure in the process of learning. Researchers working in math found that, when working with new knowledge, students given *less* support by their teacher and asked to work collaboratively with each other significantly outperformed classmates who were given a traditional, scaffolded lesson with teacher support on follow-up evaluations. They identified three key characteristics to achieve what they call *productive failure:* ensure the work is challenging but not to the level of frustration, provide learners time to communicate about what they are doing, and give students a chance to assess good and bad solutions to the problems to deepen their understanding (Kapur & Bielaczyc, 2012).

In many ways, this makes perfect sense. Deep understanding comes from genuinely working through an idea, understanding how it relates to things we already know, and being clear about what it *is* and what it *is not*. By taking away this vital work, teachers are reducing both student understanding and the development of resilience, which comes from facing and overcoming adversity. Students are both less knowledgeable and less competent when we are too involved.

Where Do I Begin?

Regrettably, failure has received a bad rap in education and is seen as a negative rather than a potentially powerful learning opportunity. Here are some thoughts on how you can start to use failure in a more productive way in your classroom.

Redefine failure. Help students understand that failure is a crucial part of the learning process and is vital to their success. Failure is the beginning of an opportunity to do things better. I heard of a teacher who used to bring in photos of her baking failures, which were numerous, to share with her students. This demonstrated that she struggled with her own learning. The students would celebrate with her when she had a success, which they recognized was hard won. This sent a message to students about the importance of resilience and commitment.

Don't jump in too early. Our impatience to stick to self-imposed timelines means that we often don't give students the time they need to work through something. If we cut their thinking off too early and then give them the answer, we are training them to be reliant. We need to recognize that our rushed approach and our desire to prevent students from struggling are having unintended negative consequences on our students by not allowing them to work through the entire learning and thinking processes.

Allow do-overs. More often than not in life, we continue to work on our work and get better. This doesn't mean that we work endlessly with students redoing an assignment countless times, but it does mean we can work more strategically with them. Working on continuous improvement is the very essence of the learning process and something that we often miss if we are overly focused on final evaluations rather than the more important formative assessments. A do-over means that the learning is continuing. Try to allow them when it's practical to do so.

Overcoming Obstacles

Changing this perspective will take some time. Here are some ways to respond to common challenges.

Students are having a hard time looking at failure as an opportunity. This is quite natural. It is engrained into students from a young age that failure is the worst thing that can happen in school and means they are stupid, lazy, or both. However, fear is not a sustainable or healthy motivator. Changing your outlook on failure may take time. It may also put you at odds with other teachers the students have. This is okay, too. Understanding that there is more than one way to do things is an important lesson for students. Engaging students in longer-term projects with multiple opportunities for success and failure will help them to understand that they can overcome problems with creativity, flexibility, perseverance, and compromise.

Students' parents are having a hard time looking at failure as an opportunity. It's important to explain to parents why you are doing things differently. Most parents have experienced a perceived failure at some point in their lives and understand how important it is for their child to learn how to manage these challenges. In my experience, most parents are excited by this kind of work once they have a clear understanding of why you are doing things differently and why that's better for the child. Parents value creative teachers who are genuinely trying to make learning more engaging for their children, and they can be important allies in the work.

Change the Environment to Change the Learner

Brenna Lamprey, a 5th grade teacher, and Beth Reilly, a preschool special education teacher, paired up to meet the needs of both older and younger students. After learning about autism spectrum disorders, the grade 5 students began to visit with the preschool students. The 5th graders were challenged to plan lessons to meet the developmental needs of the younger students. The older students then helped prepare some of the younger students to participate in a Special Olympics program by attending their physical education class once a week to help them develop their skills. The ideas continued to build, with guest speakers coming into the class to talk about other disabilities, students engaging in a research project, and finally, students planning a schoolwide Exceptional Students Week.

While the work had a very positive impact for the preschool students, it was equally influential on the 5th graders. According to Lamprey and Reilly, "16 out of 21 fifth-grade students increased their scores on the empathy survey given at the beginning and end of the school year. Some even doubled their score. The impact that the buddies had on each other not only changed attitudes and biases, but had a positive effect on their daily interactions with younger children, peers, and adults" (Lamprey & Reilly, 2016).

Student behavior tends to be very contextual. Because of their preoccupation with social relationships, peers, and status, students are likely even more focused on their environment and how others around them react to it. The traditional school environment sends a lot of unintended, implicit messages about learning to students: It is a quiet, passive process that is done on paper, with beginning and end times, for the purpose of being evaluated at the end based on someone else's expectations of what you should have learned. Outside school, we see different kinds of learning and development taking place.

For example, we asked a couple of boys at my school who were not particularly engaged in learning if they wanted to help a teacher clean up a garden at the front of the school. The garden was in a traffic turnaround, highly visible, and badly overgrown. The boys gave up many volunteer hours to the project, worked in the rain, asked to work extra hours, and ended up doing a great job. Equally interesting was that their behavior in class improved as a result of this project. Somehow, the relevance of the work, the pride they took in it, and the ability to see the fruits of their labor changed their behavior even after they were done.

So what else is going on there? What else do we know about learning and the environment that could help us shape the organization and culture of our schools?

Where Do I Begin?

The good news is that the classroom environment can be changed in a way to elicit much more positive results; students' adaptation to the environment can be used to promote positive change just as easily as it can negatively affect learning. It is thus necessary to change the environment if we want to see different behaviors. Here are some thoughts about what this looks like.

Create the environment you want students to adapt to. Many of the traditions of the classroom are not well suited to promoting deep learning: The artificial division of subjects makes it hard for student to see connections; strict time limits can stop students from developing ideas by forcing them to work in periods that are too short; and having teachers work independently from each other rather than collaborate means that the various parts of most students' days are disjointed and discontinuous. While many of these factors may be difficult to control at the individual teacher level and will, over time, require more widespread retooling of educational structures, beginning the move toward more learning-focused structures at the classroom level is a necessary first step.

It's basic biology that animals will adapt to their environments (and change them, too). If you start to think about your classroom as a learning ecosystem, how can you change the environment to change the learner? Figure 4.1 offers some ideas to get you started.

FIGURE 4.1	
Creating the Environment	
Desired State	**Environment That Will Create the State**
I want students to take more responsibility for their work.	Give the students more control over their learning to increase their drive and sense of pride through ownership.
I want students to make more effort.	Engage them with work that has genuine, real-world purpose so that they are motivated to do their best.
I want students to see school as purposeful and positive.	Give them meaningful work to do so that they derive a sense of personal satisfaction from it.
I want students to take initiative in the class-room.	Create a classroom where students are actively encouraged to make decisions, take the lead, and partner with you to enhance learning.
I want students to work together collabora-tively.	Get students into learning pods and out of seated rows so that they can interact more easily.
I want to do less grading, and I want the quality of student work to be better so that grading is easier.	Have students working on richer, lengthier tasks, which frees you up to spend time in conversation and observation with them while making anecdotal notes about what they know and can do. Give them purposeful products to create for an audience so that they make their best effort.
I want students to take more responsibility for the classroom itself.	Give groups sections of the room to be responsible for and give students input into the organization and layout of the room. They will take better care of a space if they feel that it is really theirs.

Prioritize learning over traditional structures. Much of the way school is done is based on how it has been done in the past. Looking for new opportunities to rethink our structures to enhance learning becomes vitally important. While major educational change will take time, there are small ways that we can start to reexamine our relationship with students and learning.

Our high school classes typically last for one semester each, which meant that the students who became so engaged with the 3D printer project were supposed to finish their course in January. When three of them desperately wanted to continue their work into the second semester, we did some research and found a curriculum that fit what they wanted to do perfectly, and we made a course section for Nick, Austin, and Kyle. I oversaw the course, and we used technology to collaborate and track the work they were doing, but they largely drove the course. They were given the overall expectations and were told to collate evidence of their learning–be it meeting notes, short videos, photographs, or written journals–as they went. We connected regularly, they logged their hours, and they learned well outside the usual range of expectations for a course.

At the end of the course, the three students created a video where they went through the overall curricular expectations and explained how they demonstrated them, what they did well, what they struggled with, and how they would do better next time.

Overcoming Obstacles

Changing the environment can make students uncertain about classroom behavior. Here are some possible challenges and tips on how to manage them.

Behavioral issues have increased as the classroom environment has changed. It's important to give students time to adjust to changes. It's not desirable, for example, to change everything at once. Make one deliberate change at a time, prioritized by what you think will create the most benefit. It's also crucial to have a conversation with students about why you think it will be better and what behavior in the new context will look like. The most likely way to end up in trouble is to not lay out adequate groundwork when making a change. When students understand that the change will benefit them but that they also need to adapt accordingly, they are much more likely to be both cooperative and enthusiastic about the change. It's important not to mistake learning problems for behavioral ones; oftentimes, it's the lack of a clear discussion about expectations and a feedback process that is the root of the troubles.

The classroom is noisier, and there is more movement than I am comfortable with. A classroom where students are engaged in meaningful work looks different from a traditional classroom. Part of making the changes required in our classrooms is recognizing our own biases and preconceptions. Students sitting quietly in rows completing paperwork invoke a certain degree of satisfaction for us because they are doing what they are supposed to do in a traditional model and because the classroom appears to be under control. What's most striking in this model is what's not there. Students aren't collaborating, brainstorming, challenging each other, or excited. We need to take care not to mistake compliance for engagement.

In private sector terms, we want the classroom to look more like a start-up and less like a factory floor. Students should be moving around, engaging in creative work, trying things they're not sure how to do, and debating next steps.

Resource Student Work Appropriately

One of the ways that we implicitly communicate to students the importance of their work is through the resources that we use to support that work. Part of changing the educational environment is reallocating the resources of the environment.

Typically, schools have a certain number of resources available to them, the majority of them controlled by adults:

- Human resources: the students, staff, parents, and volunteers in the building
- Financial resources: money in the school budget or available from outside sources
- Time: the way the day is structured
- Space: the physical building that the school occupies and the property it resides on
- Technology: both the technology that students carry with them on a daily basis and the technology available through the school or potential partners
- Community resources: access to resources in the areas surrounding the school

In looking at this list, it's interesting to reflect on what messages, implicit and explicit, schools send to students. Time, for example, is a resource that in most schools is controlled almost exclusively by the adults (outside of recess and lunch, which are, not coincidentally, the best part of the day for many students). The unequal distribution and focus of resources send implicit messages to students about where they fit into the hierarchy of the school.

By shifting teachers into the role of supporters, cheerleaders, problem solvers, and resource hunters, we are shifting the human resources in the building to *support* student learning rather than *direct* it. By giving students access to some funding, we can teach them that their work is worthwhile and about the importance of budgeting, thinking creatively, and being judicious with their money. By giving students space and time in the school that can be used for collaboration and student-driven work, we let them know that we value those things. By providing students access to technology that enhances their ability to create, collaborate, and publish, we highlight the significance of this work while also teaching them about the potential of technology beyond social media and gaming. By helping students find community resources to support their work, we are telling them that the world outside the school also cares about their learning.

Where Do I Begin?

Here are some areas to begin with to resource student work appropriately.

Provide students the human resources to do their work. By supporting student work rather than directing it, you make yourself an important resource for students. Schools are full of energetic, creative people—think about how other staff and students in the school could be resources. Are there opportunities to pair up with other classes to engage in cross-curricular work? Are there other staff members, volunteers, and community members who can help? Looking at the school as a community of support to aid in student work means that students can tap into vast amounts of potential energy.

Try to find sources of funding to support students' work. The chance to provide students some funding, and the accompanying lessons about money management, can create great supplementary learning opportunities. Even if the funding is modest, it helps reaffirm the importance of students' work because it sends the message that it's worth being supported. Money can be hard to come by, and more so in some communities than others, but here are some options to consider:

- Student fundraising. Figuring out what they can do for free, how much money they will require, and how to raise the funds will force students to think practically about their plans. It will also help them learn important lifelong lessons about money management.
- Grants. At South Branch, students in the class applied for environmental grants. We ended up winning two for a total of two thousand dollars.

Money can often be found if the work is important and you can find tie-ins with other organizations.

- Administration. Administrators can't always provide large amounts of funding, but most will try to find something to help support student work, particularly if the work is important, meaningful to the students, and good for the broader school.
- Community. If you have an exciting and meaningful project going on, there may well be local businesses and organizations who would be happy to lend a hand. Again, the process of writing persuasive letters, preparing an inspiring pitch, and working productively with community partners can all be part of the learning process.

Redefine the use of space to support student work. Are there ways that you can give students space in the classroom for their work? Whiteboards where they can do their brainstorming and make notes are useful. Put up chart paper, project planners, and research notes. Online collaboration tools allow students to continue to collaborate even at home. Visible work is important work, so the students and anyone else coming into the classroom should be able to see what students are working on.

Ensure that students have adequate access to technology. Is there technology in the classroom dedicated specifically to student work? To what extent are students permitted and encouraged to use their own technology to advance the work they are doing? For most adults, it's hard to imagine doing work of importance without any kind of technology integration, and that's equally true for students. While technology has the potential to be a distraction, when students have work that is driven by them, has meaning, and is important, you dramatically reduce the risk of them using the technology inappropriately. It's also important to remember that even a basic computer with a browser and internet access can allow students nearly unlimited access to information, resources, and applications.

Look to community resources to help students with their work. What governmental or private resources exist in the community that could support the work of students? In many cases, students can be coached to contact potential partners themselves, an important skill that is not frequently integrated into school. How do you succinctly tell someone what you are looking for and convince them to help you? How can you frame discussions with community partners around win-win scenarios, recognizing that a longer-term, deeper relationship will be dependent on both sides benefiting from the relationship? Many community organizations, individuals, and companies will be all too happy to help. The principal reason that more groups are not involved with schools is that schools frequently struggle to create space for them.

Overcoming Obstacles

Resourcing student work in schools with lots of resources is easier than in one with limited resources. Here are some thoughts on this challenge.

The school has very limited resources available. Unfortunately, there can be a huge range in available resources. Some schools seem to have almost limitless resources, while others have very few.

Thinking creatively about the resources you do have available to you is important, as is focusing on what you have rather than what you don't have. You may, for example, have limited financial resources but perhaps have more access to human resources. In some cases, one resource can be used to increase the amount of another; for example, if you have reasonable human resources, you could organize a fundraiser to provide more access to technology. It's also the case that many businesses are looking for opportunities to do good things with their money, and an inspiring story connected to an ambitious program might be just the thing to get the ball rolling on some additional funds. There are also many grants available to support various types of student work, and schools with limited resources may be the most likely to win them. Invite students to participate in the application process by using it as part of their work on persuasive writing to turn the process into a learning experience.

Remember that even small changes in the allocation of resources will send an important message to students. Changing students' perceptions of the significance of their work is just as valuable as providing substantial resources.

Model Lifelong Learning

Ask teachers what they want their students to come away with from their schooling, and becoming a lifelong learner is almost always on the short list. Unfortunately, traditional schooling can be a disincentive to this goal because the implicit messaging is that learning is something you do because you have to, not because you are self-motivated to do so. What's also unfortunate is that some teachers have changed very little in their classrooms over the last decade, which means they are not modeling lifelong learning, even when they recognize its importance.

Where Do I Begin?

How do we begin to shift the dynamic in the classroom to ensure that we are graduating the lifelong learners that we all want to see? Here are some starting points.

Talk to students about what *you* are learning. Do your students see you as a learner? Do they know that you read and attend professional development on how to get better as an educator? Do they know that you have interests and passions outside school that you are also learning about?

The fact is that students need good learning role models. Taking time in class to talk about what you are learning, and in turn what they are learning in their nonschool lives, will lead to deeper relationships and a better understanding of who you are as a group. It may also lead to additional jumping-off points for real-world learning in your classroom.

Model failure. Teachers work very hard to ensure that they don't make mistakes, but the unintended offshoot of this effort is to give students a sense that teachers simply don't make them. If students are not sure about how to do something, they ask the teacher and the teacher tells them. This air of infallibility promotes a fixed mindset, holds teachers back from taking the necessary risks involved with classroom innovation, and deprives students and teachers of the wonderful opportunity to learn that failure provides.

Model risk taking. Do students know when you are trying something new? Have you explained to them why you are doing something differently than you've done before? Letting a class know that "last time I tried this lesson, it was a real flop" or "I just read about this new idea that sounds really interesting, but I've never done this before" is a great way to communicate with students that even as an adult you are continuing to try to get better and that it doesn't always work.

Ask students for help. When a new idea flops, as they sometimes will, ask students what they think went wrong. Tell them what you learned from the experience and ask them how you could change it so it might work next time. Bring the idea back the next day and say, "I've made some changes. Let's try this again."

Try new ideas more than once. Lots of teachers have come back from a conference with a new idea, tried it once, and abandoned it when classroom behavior became more challenging because "It doesn't work!" Recognizing that most worthwhile things aren't achieved the first time, making some changes, and coming back to an idea again give us the opportunity to model resilience.

Overcoming Obstacles

Remember that setting a good example for students is in this area is vital and probably not as much work as you might fear.

Teachers don't have time in class to model lifelong learning and risk taking. If you think about it, it's really something you are doing anyway; all this strategy is recommending is that you let students into the discussion. It's worth taking the time to nurture it, particularly if we insist that it is one of the system's top priorities.

Taking It to the Next Level

As you become more comfortable with how to create space to learn, here is one more idea about where to take the work.

Involve students in a classroom redesign. One visual way to demonstrate student ownership in the classroom is to work with them to redesign the space. Far more than an exercise in simply redecorating, it creates an opportunity to discuss how the space is a resource that should reflect the work. Should the class look like a traditional classroom, or should it have different types of spaces reflective of the learning that is taking place? There's a good chance that students need places to meet, tech centers, places for quiet work, and places to be creative. What does the classroom space tell you about the expectations for behavior? Is it laid out to maximize the visibility of a teacher at the center of the room, or is it reflective of a space where teams work together to accomplish a wide variety of goals? Does it look like a lecture hall or a workshop? Physical space sends messages about behavior, so it is important to engage students in this discussion.

Reflection

When creating spaces to learn, here are some questions that can be used at the beginning of the process and as you start to make progress:

- Do students know what *you* are learning? Do they know what you want to learn next?
- Do you know what your students want to learn? Do you know what they are learning currently outside school?

- How do students share their learning goals? How do other students and the teacher help them to achieve these goals?
- Are students currently excited about learning in your class?
- In a typical day, how much control do students have over their learning? How much autonomy, mastery, and purpose do they have?
- Do your students currently see failure as an opportunity to get better?
- What does your current timetable and structure of the day say to students about the amount of input they have?
- Are your current classroom structures and practices enhancing or detracting from the behavior and learning experiences you would like to see from your students?
- Do students have the resources they need to complete meaningful work? If not, how could those resources enhanced?
- How much control do students have over classroom resources?

Final Thoughts

Looking back on the experience of the 3D printer group, we acknowledge that not everything went perfectly. The business part of the students' plan was not a huge success. They had difficulty making decisions, had trouble getting enough cases printed, and frequently spread themselves too thin (a common experience for many start-ups). These issues ended up being one of the greatest sources of learning for them. In the end, their ability to train others and build up the next generation of 3D print enthusiasts was far more significant than their financial accomplishments.

Interviewing the students after the course was over, our experiment concluded, here is some of what they said: "We succeeded and we failed, and in life that's really prominent, but in school it's hard to come by. The course was realistic because we did fail at various times. We had to overcome that, and we didn't have anyone else to pick us up. We had to learn to move past it."

Another student added, "I put more work into this course than any other course, and I produced better results. Doesn't that tell you something about the education system itself?"

As a learning experience, it was clearly a huge success. Creating space for students to find themselves, and ultimately creating a space customized to them, enabled them to pursue their passions within the bounds of a high school diploma in an unconventional way.

One of the real challenges of creating space in a classroom is coming to terms with how it changes our role as the teacher. The space that we are giving to students is, essentially, space that we are currently filling. This is not a particularly easy shift for schools or teachers. The example above is perhaps at the more extreme end of what is possible, but it is a look into what schooling could look like down the road, and it was accomplished within the bounds of a regular school without profoundly altering the school's basic DNA. It also shows that when we create space, there's no telling how students might fill it. The fact is that these students dramatically surpassed every expectation that we had for them because they had the room to drive their own learning. If they had been told that they would have to start a business, train dozens of other students and staff, and consult with an expert overseas about an aspect of their project on the first day of class, their parents would have been calling the school to complain about the teacher's unreasonable demands. However, left to their own devices, and driven by their passion, this is exactly what they did.

This notion of connecting learning to the wider world outside the classroom is what we will discuss in more detail in the next chapter.

(5)

Connect Student Work
to the Community

Step 4: Connect Student Work to the Community

The Big Ideas

- Form community partnerships.

- Give students an audience.

- Recognize the social nature of learning.

- Embrace competition.

- Take students into the community.

Activation Questions

How many community partners are you currently working with?

To what extent are you taking advantage of the resources located in your neighborhood to enhance student learning?

How frequently do you take students into the community or bring the community into the classroom?

While I was at the Upper Canada District School Board, we ran boardwide entrepreneurial competitions that have led to some remarkable student projects. The competitions embody the strategies of making meaning central, creating space for learning, and contextualizing the curriculum. They also connect students to the broader community.

The Venture Education competitions are based on a popular TV format (in the United States, the show is called *Shark Tank* and in Canada it's known as *Dragons' Den*). In the shows, would-be entrepreneurs and small business owners pitch their ideas to a group of deep-pocketed businesspeople for a chance to convince them to invest in their company. There are often difficult negotiations, hard questions, and sometimes a successful investment. Our versions are far more supportive but maintain some of the central elements of the show.

In grades 4–6 and 7–8, students participate in the Change the World Challenge; high school students participate in the Innovation Challenge. The younger students are challenged to build a project that has a benefit to the wider world; what that looks like, exactly, is up to them. In the high school competition, students are encouraged to start a business, be it a for-profit or not-for-profit.

We bring the participating teams together for the day in a large workshop. For both competitions, the students are taken through the same process that looks like this:

- Student teams of four to five, plus their teacher supervisor, are brought together for the initial planning day. Students are told that the teachers are there for support and not to do the work for them. In some cases, the team is representative of an entire class or an entire division who are also involved in the project.

- The teams have the rules of the competitions and criteria explained (they are judged, e.g., on communication, the amount of progress they've made, the environmental sustainability of what they are doing, and whether they have developed community partnerships). Generally, teams have a maximum of 10 minutes to pitch their ideas and another 5 minutes to answer judges' questions.

- They are told that they can win up to $500 to support their projects at the grade 4 to 6 level, $750 at grades 7 and 8, and up to $1,000 at the high school level. The money comes from funding designated to promote innovation.

- Letting them know the competition will be broadcast over the internet adds excitement as it allows students to publish their work in a very real way to a wide audience. In our case, the broadcast lets parents, classes, and in some cases whole schools log in to cheer them on. It also allows other students involved in the projects, who weren't on the presentation team, to see how their team did in the competition.

At this point in the proceedings, the room is buzzing. If the students were kind of excited coming to the workshop, they are now really fired up. Five hundred dollars sounds like a million dollars when you are 10 years old. Being broadcast on the internet? Well, you might as well be on prime-time TV. There is a lot of nervous excitement, but it's positive in that students are feeling that (1) this is a big deal and (2) this is going to be a lot of fun.

The rest of the planning day looks like this:

- Students are taken through a brainstorming session and a project planner that they can use to organize their ideas.

- They are introduced to a basic business planning template that they need to complete for the competition. There are only five major headings, but it pushes them to think about the range of considerations required when launching a successful venture or small business.

- We teach them how to do a SWOT (strengths/weaknesses/opportunities/threats) analysis, which is a common business school tool that encourages them to use critical thinking to evaluate and improve their ideas.

- Students are shown the curriculum and need to come up with a list of curriculum expectations that they are going to demonstrate through their projects that their teachers can use for evaluation purposes (a strategy we discussed in step 2).

At this point they're sent on their way, brimming with ideas and excitement. The students return 8 to 10 weeks later (the three age groups each attend a different competition), often wearing a team uniform, to pitch their ideas.

So what do students come up with when given an open-ended challenge of this nature? The results are always a surprise.

Form Community Partnerships

There are lots of people and organizations interested in helping schools. The problem is that the insular nature of the traditional model of schooling, where things are very much classroom- and paper-based, is not well suited to taking advantage of the resources that surround the school. It often means that even when community members approach schools directly with interesting propositions, schools are not sure how to take advantage of them or attach them to the curriculum. Thinking creatively about the social and ecological context of the school is a good place to start to change that.

Where Do I Begin?

Changing the vision of the school as a sole entity to one that exists within a much bigger environment is important. The first step is to start to look at the community as an underutilized learning resource.

Identify the opportunities. Think about the organizations and people in your community who might be able to help with the work you are doing. Start close by.

On a map, draw a circle around your school three miles in diameter. How many people, businesses, other schools, institutions, green spaces, historical sites, recreational facilities, types of land use, and biomes exist within that circle? Start by listing them and reflect, in a broad sense, on how they could drive student learning (remember, as we discussed in Chapter 3, to start with the big idea and then look for curricular connections afterward). There's a very good chance that there are a large number of opportunities near your doorstep. Pulling the curriculum into your consideration, as well as the developmental stage of your students, will help you begin to refine the list and identify some key opportunities to explore.

Lay a solid groundwork for the partnership. It's not uncommon for teachers to have experienced situations where they've tried some kind of partnership or visit and it hasn't worked out as planned. Clear communication ahead of time about expectations and timelines is important. Here are some things to consider when establishing a community partnership:

1. **Ensure that you have clearly established, in writing, what you are committing to and what the partner is committing to.** This doesn't require a formal contract, but being clear about what each side is providing and when they are doing so is important to the success of the partnership.

2. **Remember to give the partner the information they need to be successful.** This may seem self-evident, but often partnerships get into trouble because we, as educators, assume that everyone knows what we know about students; it's easy to forget how much professional knowledge we have.

   For example, if you have a student with learning needs in the classroom who may be disruptive, it's important for your guest speaker to know that the student should be ignored when he does that, if that's the strategy that you and the parents are using to modify the behavior.

Partners with a lot of knowledge that they want to share may have a natural tendency to want to speak at length to their audience. Helping them to build a more interactive lesson plan will make the experience more satisfying both for the students and for them.

3. **Be clear about the roles of the adults and students in the learning.** If part of your goal is to establish student-centered, real-world learning in your classroom, your community partners should know this, too. If the role you want them to play is that of a resource to support student work, then they need to know that and will likely need a clear explanation of the broader project. Asking the partner to teach the students about a river system is a lot different than asking them to answer student questions about the components of the system because students have been challenged to improve the health of the river and its tributaries.

When Walter Bracken STEAM Academy Elementary School in Las Vegas, Nevada, started a large gardening program, they went to the community to help them, partnering with nonprofits, the community, and large major retailers alike. The school's principal, Kathleen Decker (2016), offers these helpful tips on creating successful partnerships:

- Start with a vision of a project that can include hands-on support from the community. It can be a garden, a school makeover, murals, or adding trees.

- Reach out to local groups, service organizations, and businesses who may have a shared interest and ideas about how they can help, remembering that materials and a helping hand can sometimes be easier to ask for than money.

- Celebrate the completion of your project with a ribbon-cutting event that can even include your local Chamber of Commerce, and continue to invite your community partners back to keep them engaged.

Make use of volunteers. While many schools are good at having volunteers to support reading programs, this tends to drop off dramatically in older grades. This is probably a mistake. There are many learners in our classrooms who could benefit from help and contact time with other caring adults, and there are plenty of people in our communities with the experience and education to help.

Like with other kinds of partnerships, the most important thing here is to ensure that you've laid a solid groundwork. Taking time to train volunteers and provide them with some documentation will help ensure that they are doing what's needed in the way you want them to. While this requires some investment in time, the longer-term payoff can be tremendous.

Overcoming Obstacles

Unfortunately, community partnerships can sometimes seem hard to come by, and they don't always go as planned. Here are some ways to deal with potential issues.

This rural school has limited potential community connections. It can be more of a challenge to use the three-mile circle exercise described earlier if you work in a largely rural school district. That said, rural communities are often very community-minded, which means that people and organizations in them are likely to want to help. Remember that people can come to you; you don't always have to go to them.

For example, one of the high schools in our board is located next to a cemetery, has an elementary school across the road, and is otherwise located in the middle of farm country. This might seem somewhat limited as far as community resources go, but there are in fact many opportunities even on this short list. One could even use all three together: Students could use the cemetery to identify people from the community to conduct historical research, meet with a farmer to understand how rural lives have changed over time, and then create a children's book about the people they were studying and the time they lived in to read to students at the elementary school across the road. This would simultaneously give students a better understanding of the past, provide them deeper connections to the community, and allow them to spread these connections and knowledge by sharing them with younger students while using multiple curricular expectations.

The partnership is not meeting teachers' expectations. Pre-planning and following the suggestions above are the best way to avoid getting into this situation. It's important that you have a clear discussion with your partner and that everyone knows what they have committed to. If you follow the recommendations, it will become apparent early in the process if there are irreconcilable differences in the planning discussions. If, despite good planning, things are still not working properly, there are two viable options:

- Sit down with the partner and discuss your concerns, with a focus on how you think the partnership could be improved (rather than from an angle of criticizing what has been happening). With some goodwill and honesty, you should be able to get things back on track.

- Remember that this is your classroom. In the end, you are the one who will decide what the students will do, whether the process is successful, and whether you will continue with the partnership or not. Ultimately, you hold the authority for the learning in the classroom and should never feel beholden to a partner with strong opinions that run contrary to yours.

Our partnership is not going well, and I think we're going to have to end it. Sometimes, despite our best planning, things do not go as well as we hoped. Invite the partner to conference with you to see how they think things are going; they may also see some areas for improvement. If you still can't make it work, then end the partnership and look for another option.

Ending a partnership that isn't working is not a negative thing. In fact, use this as a lesson with students to discuss how we determine when things just aren't working, why we end a partnership, and how we do so respectfully and amicably. It's important to teach students that staying focused on our goals and changing directions when things are not working well are crucial to finding eventual success. Model appropriate communication skills, like how to negotiate productively or how to write an effective thank you letter.

Give Students an Audience

Middle school students in South Carolina were challenged to use design thinking to build transitional housing for the homeless using shipping pallets and to create a plan for a transitional housing community. Their plans were submitted to a local development group that was, effectively, doing the same thing. The group judged the students' plans and provided feedback based on their knowledge of these communities nationally. One student commented, "Never in my life did I think that I'd be building a house . . . especially one that can be used to help the homeless. And we're just kids! This is amazing!" (Riddle, 2016).

One of the ways to communicate to students that their work is important is through sharing it. While it is obviously not appropriate for all student work to be public, saying to students that "This work is worth sharing" sends the message that their work is substantial and important.

Students who are struggling and disengaged from school and aim only to pass have limited motivation to do any better if the work itself does not leave them feeling confident and proud of their accomplishments. Students need to be engaged in work that is (1) important enough to be shared and (2) shared with a wider community. For example, all of the students who competed in the Venture Education competitions were graded on the work they did (largely on the curriculum expectations they selected themselves), but the work involved in preparing for the competition, building connections in the community, solving problems, and collaborating in meaningful ways was far more important.

When our students in the South Branch project (Chapter 2) were told that they were all going to be contributing to newspaper articles that would be read regionwide as part of their project to reduce the environmental footprint of the community, they worked harder on the editing than almost anything else that year. The grading came afterward, and the students did extremely well—far better than I had seen classes do in the past when they were told to write a newspaper report to be read only by me.

Making student work important means challenging students with work that is designed to be shared and has value in itself. Learning and doing are the primary motivators; the evaluation at the end doesn't create meaning, nor does it inspire the best work from students.

The Change the World Challenge has had local TV personalities, a former mayor, and people who have worked overseas in development as judges, which adds additional excitement to the day. The Innovation Challenge has had many successful local entrepreneurs as judges, as well as people who work in economic development and the not-for-profit sector (e.g., one of our judges started her own school). Because they understand that we are working with children, the judges are far less prickly than the ones you see on TV, but they still ask the students thoughtful questions about their proposals and provide meaningful feedback and encouragement.

Because the competitions were broadcast live over the internet, classes involved in the projects, and in some cases entire schools, were able to cheer on the students, who returned to accolades from their classmates and teachers.

While not everything that students do in school needs to be public, giving them periodic opportunities to share their learning on a bigger stage can bring out the best in students and teach them how to manage the pressure of public work.

Where Do I Begin?

When considering what kind of audience to offer your students, it's important to keep several elements in mind.

Find the biggest audience appropriate to your students' age and stage. Think about your own reactions to the following prompt. Your principal asks you to consider sharing something interesting you are doing in your classroom:

- With two of your colleagues.
- With the entire staff of your school.
- At a boardwide professional development session.
- At a national education conference.

While each escalation might promote an increasing sense of anxiety and excitement, note the message that the principal is sending to you about the importance of the work you are doing as you are moving further up the scale; if your principal thinks what you're doing is worthy of a national conference, she must really think it's amazing. Consider also how much time and effort you would put into preparing to share with a couple of colleagues versus running a workshop on a national stage. In the first case, you might spend time reviewing your notes or digging through some student work to share. In the second case, you would likely put countless hours into writing, revising, field-testing ideas, and consulting with a range of colleagues about what you were going to share. This is because important work is our best work. And the same is true for students.

There are, of course, limits. We would not expect most students to be comfortable on a national stage at an early age, nor is this necessary. If the level of risk in the audience is raised to a point of outright fear, then it's too ambitious. If in doubt, start with a smaller audience, and if things go well, look to expand it outward. Like other work you are doing with them, remember that preparing for an audience can also be scaffolded. An evening presentation to the parents of the class might start with a visit from the teacher next door or a presentation to another class, with an opportunity for constructive audience feedback and reflection. Articles bound for internet publication might go through a few rounds of peer editing. An interview with local media could be rehearsed and filmed with another adult with media experience, giving students an opportunity to practice thinking on their feet and anticipating questions. We don't ask students to publish a short story before we've spent time working on paragraphs. Students should walk before they run when it comes to audiences, too.

Take work students are currently doing and give it an audience. Realistically, not every assignment that you give has to be intrinsically meaningful. However, if students are going to spend a lot of time on something, then the work needs to be important, and important work is shared. Start by trying to modify a major project you are currently doing. Here are two starting questions:

- Does the project currently make sense outside the educational context? Would someone *not* in a school, for example, recognize that what the students are doing is important? If not, how could you modify it to signify to students that the work is important?
- How can you share the work publicly (online, in the community, or even in other parts of the school)?
  - ➤ Publishing by producing a newspaper, magazine, blog, wiki, or display of student work. Creating a class Facebook, Instagram, YouTube, or Twitter account to share student learning (while keeping in mind privacy concerns).
  - ➤ Sharing the work with other students or staff in the school through workshops, assemblies, performances, or campaigns.
  - ➤ Inviting members of the broader community to see what students have been working on by organizing community events or open houses.

The chances are that students are already doing work that could allow you to experiment with audience in your classroom. You may be amazed to see how the addition of audience can increase motivation, which will drive improved performance.

Prioritize publishing over grading. This one sounds a little counterintuitive because we often make the mistaken assumption that school is about creating work for grading rather than learning, but think about the evaluation of student work as secondary to the actual sharing of the work. This is the difference between writing a report on the environment and promoting and organizing the cleanup of a local creek while generating media interest and educating the wider community about its importance. The principal purpose of the first one is to generate a grade. The principal purpose of the second is to improve the community. In both cases there will be an opportunity to evaluate student knowledge of ecosystems, but students are going to be far more engaged and take the learning far more seriously in the second case. It's also going to be a lot more fun to evaluate.

This is an important indicator to remember: If students are handing in poor-quality work, there's a good chance that the intrinsic importance of the work is not obvious to them.

Keep safety in mind. It's obviously crucial that appropriate safety considerations are taken when planning an audience or publishing widely. Most school boards have clear policies about how and where information about students can be shared. Using first names only, avoiding photographs, and protecting the identity of specific students can usually be accommodated easily. Remember, the focus is on the learning more than the student, so think about how to share the work without sharing the details of the student in case there are specific concerns.

Overcoming Obstacles

Because students are accustomed to the private nature of school work, giving them an audience will be an adjustment for them. Here are some strategies to help manage the transition.

Students are intimidated by the prospect of sharing their work. This is both a common issue and totally natural. There *is* something intimidating about sharing work with an audience, but that's part of the point. The private exchange of documentation that underlies most student work is of such low risk that, for some students, it means they make very little effort. Sharing the work on a larger scale is initially intimidating, but part of the role of a school is to push the limits of students, challenge them, and help them learn that they are capable of more than they thought. Encouraging their best work by arranging for an audience, showing them how to prepare effectively, and talking them through how we, as adults, work through intimidating situations is vital to their future success. It's also clear that students won't get more comfortable with sharing their work if they never do it. Think how much better prepared students would be for job interviews if they regularly made presentations, received feedback, and improved their oral skills and ability to think on their feet in school. Think about how much better prepared students would be in a pitch to find funding for a business if they had experienced making pitches and getting feedback from local business owners while still in school. Think about how much easier it would be for students to get involved with local politics later on if they had been involved with partnering with their local municipality to design a skateboard park.

A parent is not comfortable with the idea of sharing student work with an audience. Unfortunately, this is an all-too-common occurrence these days. Explain the purpose of sharing the work and the multitude of additional skills that having an audience brings to work being done. Let parents know that there will be opportunities to practice and get feedback, their apprehension is natural, and working through that discomfort is part of the process.

If some accommodations need to be made, try to come up with a plan that will maximize the skill acquisition while still meeting their needs. The goal is not to embarrass students or raise safety concerns if there are circumstances requiring a high degree of privacy. As mentioned earlier, leaving student names and photos out and letting the work stand on its own is an easy way to separate the work from its creators.

Recognize the Social Nature of Learning

Thanks to a bike repair program run by Warren Collegiate in Warren, Manitoba, students were able to work together to help others in the community. The students learned about local bike shops that promoted positive social change by providing disadvantaged individuals with a means of transportation, improving fitness, and promoting recycling all at the same time. After two days of training, students began to repair and donate bikes to community groups and individuals. Their social circle expanded even further when they volunteered to help repair and donate bikes to a local summer camp to benefit even more young people in the community. They also worked with younger students to pass along the skills that they had learned so that the program could expand and continue (EcoLeague, 2016).

Why is the importance of work driven, in part, by its public nature? Because humans are social learners, and the bigger the social context, the more important the work is perceived to be. That's not to say that there isn't a great deal of work that is done out of the limelight. However, if our intention is to teach students that what they are doing is important, we need to build a social context for that work. Regularly limiting student work to paperwork shared privately with the teacher, while appropriate at times, inadvertently encourages poor quality and sends messages that the work is not important. Publishing their work in some form is far more realistic to the way that students are likely to live their lives after school. How many adults have jobs where their sole responsibility is to complete paperwork for a single individual?

The influential American writer John Dewey went to great lengths to describe the inherently social aspects of us as learning primates. Dewey wrote passionately and persuasively in "My Pedagogic Creed," first published in 1897, "I believe that the school must represent present life—life as real and vital to the child as that which he carries on in the home, in the neighborhood, or on the playground. I believe that education which does not occur through forms of life, forms that are worth living for their own sake, is always a poor substitute for the genuine reality, and tends to cramp and to deaden."

Over a century later, the creed continues to make for powerful reading. It is striking to see how many of the concepts being discussed today are not new. Bringing learning into a broader social context is, thus, crucial to student engagement and success. We need to learn and demonstrate our learning in social contexts because that is fundamentally what we are: social learners.

One of the first steps in the Change the World Challenge and Innovation Challenge is to bring the teams together in a large hall to take them through a planning process. The social aspect of the process is purposeful. Teams are competing, but because they tend to come up with such different concepts, they are often happy to exchange ideas. They are also sharing a social experience. They are stretching their boundaries together and are nervous but excited about the possibilities. The real work is in seeing the project developed; the competition is an important motivator, but the social element of the work is even more important. This is school as present life.

Where Do I Begin?

It's not necessary, of course, to start a large-scale competition to build social learning structures. Classroom project work is a natural place to start. Here are some tips to get started.

Create teams to complete important work. In the real world, significant issues are tackled by teams of people. Big issues and problems require a wide range of involvement, skills, and individuals. Important work in class needs to be done in groups because important work in the real world is done in groups. Many of the most crucial skills students need to learn from schools are the skills required to work with others including collaborating, negotiating, carrying their weight, managing conflict, and coming to consensus.

Ensure there are roles for every student. The best teams have different roles so that all students can play a meaningful part. Helping students understand their value, as well as the value of others, is vital to their future success. Providing students distinct roles that play to their strengths—and avoid reducing them to stereotyped stronger and weaker students—will build their confidence while also ensuring accountability because their individual role can be assessed and evaluated.

Self-knowledge and understanding how we work with others can go a long way toward creating group cohesiveness. In my experience, I've used a personality questionnaire with students that determines how they tend to work in a group. Are they a process person (focused on the steps), product person (wanting to see the work done), idea person (most interested in brainstorming), or people person (focused on the feelings and sense of belonging of group members)? Spending some time talking to them about how and why they might struggle with certain group members, while also learning to value difference, will help students learn a great deal about themselves and each other.

Create the teams yourself. This one is often a source of debate, but my experience has been that it is better to create teams that you think are balanced, have a variety of role players, and have personalities that will generally get along. If one group stands out too much from the other groups, it will have a negative effect on everyone.

In the real world, we seldom have a chance to pick the teams we work on. Working with a range of personalities, getting to know people we didn't know well before, and learning to manage conflict are all important skills.

Meet with teams regularly. Part of the social element of learning is the meaningful interaction not only among the students but also with the teacher. Meet regularly with teams to help them improve their work, refine their ideas, and challenge them to go even further. This practice also sends the message to the students that their work is important, you are interested in what they are doing, and you are here to help them be their best.

Put teams on a rotation and ensure that they have specific deliverables with due dates to help keep them on track. It's also wise to set up the meeting rotation so that you meet more frequently with groups that are struggling to get traction. Like individual students, groups of students require differentiated instruction.

Overcoming Obstacles

Group work can have its share of challenges. Here are some strategies you can use to help address them.

Students in a group are not getting along. It is important to acknowledge problems and then help students find solutions to them. Coming back to the personality profile questionnaire you used can be helpful because many of them include tips on how different types of people can work together.

Helping students to identify the real source of conflict is also crucial. Sometimes when they say, "I don't like them," what they are really saying is, "I have a different vision for the project" or "I want to use a different process." Moving students toward a discussion that is about the work, rather than focusing on personal conflicts, can help them move forward. This is also why meeting with groups regularly is important so that you can monitor potential issues and head them off before they become a major problem.

Not getting along with groupmates is one of the main reasons that some students don't like working in a group. The fact is that it is hard work but also entirely necessary. It is a crucial life skill.

One group is struggling in their project. Differentiating and spending different amounts of time with groups is entirely reasonable. In my experience, groups will often go through stages where they are unsure what to do next, and others where they have great focus and drive and know exactly what they are all doing. Spending more time with some groups who are at an impasse is perfectly acceptable.

The rest of the class can be a resource here. If a group is stuck, they can present the work they've done and have the rest of the class provide feedback and ideas. This process can also help reinforce to the students that the struggle is part of the work and is not a personal reflection of them.

Some students are working harder than others. The issue of different members of a group making differing amounts of effort is a common one. The trouble educators get into is when we give every student in the group the same grade, knowing full well that it's not representative of their individual efforts, leading to resentment and frustration.

The trick here is not to abandon group work but rather to ensure that we've structured it fairly. Garfield Gini-Newmann, a University of Toronto professor from the Critical Thinking Consortium, argues that the easiest way to do this is to ensure that each person in the group has a separate role to play and, in the end, is evaluated on that role. For example, if students are putting together a newspaper, the student in charge of the sports section would be evaluated on that section of the paper. Difficulty can be avoided by ensuring everyone has a distinct role and that they are evaluated on what they have done, and not assigned an overall group grade.

There is also potential for some peer and self-assessment here. Have group members check in, reflect on their contributions, and hear from other members of the group about their performance. As a teacher, this means carefully choosing criteria that will focus more on the work than on the individual. This is obviously not about personally criticizing classmates but rather an opportunity for students to reflect on their role in the group and the quality and quantity of the work before setting some goals for improvement.

Embrace Competition

At Hood River Middle School in Oregon, where they have a focus on bringing community partners in to make learning more relevant, the students compete in an Iron Chef competition as part of their work in the kitchen in the Food and Conservation Science program. The school brings in judges ranging from local chefs to the mayor to determine the winner, bringing a real-world edge to the competition. Students in the program also run cafés and can earn their food handler's card ("Bringing the Community," 2016).

An important piece of the Venture Education process is the value of competition. Overly broad concerns about the effects of competition on student self-esteem in schools has eliminated, to a large extent, meaningful competition in the classroom. This school of thinking sees competition as a destructive force. What it ignores, of course, is the fact that self-confidence doesn't come from pretending not to keep score in the soccer game in gym class, it comes from meaningful accomplishment. The unintentional consequence of all this focus on self-esteem appears to be the development of students who are not used to competition, have very little resilience, and have very high levels of anxiety, the exact opposite of what the focus on self-esteem had hoped to accomplish. The point is not to have students never lose; it's about learning how to handle loss and to use that knowledge to be better next time. It's not about never winning; it's about winning and learning the value of modesty and being a good sport.

The most pressing case for the appropriate use of competition, however, is the fact that students are going into a competitive world. The profound changes in the economies of the world mean that even though more students are graduating from college or university than ever before, their salaries are dropping while their student loans are skyrocketing. Students who would have happily found a middle-class lifestyle through unionized factory work are now working minimum wage jobs in the service industry. At the same time, the opportunities for today's young people have never been greater. It's possible to set up a website and online store in a day or two to sell products to people anywhere in the world. Thanks to social media, students can connect with thousands of people instantly to promote a cause, make connections that could lead to employment, or generate excitement about their start-up or idea. The world is their oyster, but only for those who think critically, collaborate widely, think pragmatically, and are not afraid of a little competition.

Competition should be used judiciously. Creating an endless string of losing situations for students is not helping them. However, making them part of a team of diverse learners, giving them an important task, and creating a competition to spur them on to do their best *is* helping them.

It's also important to note that you can make competition more or less constructive, depending on how it's structured. In our first Venture Education competitions, the judges decided that they wanted everyone to get at least some money, reasoning that all of the students had good ideas, made an effort, and were to be encouraged to pursue their ideas. This worked because it encouraged everyone to move forward while not detracting from the winners who received more money for their work. It will also encourage students to come back to the competition, eager to do even better next time. Competition doesn't have to be cutthroat; it is possible to set it up to both recognize excellence and be supportive.

Where Do I Begin?

While you may not be inclined to set up a competition like we did with Venture Education, there are plenty of ways to use competition constructively to encourage students to do their best and create excitement. Here are some tips on where to start.

Focus on using competition to drive students' best work, rather than purely on winning and losing. Discuss the benefits of winning and losing to help students gain some perspective before you start. Learning how to be good winners and good losers is a life skill that students need. By focusing on product, rather than personality, the competition is about not the students themselves but rather the fruits of their thoughts and efforts. Being able to be honest about our work, and to compare and contrast it with the work of others, is part of how we learn to improve.

In the Venture Education competition, this outcome was embodied by the number of groups who, after watching other teams make their pitch, said things like, "That's a great idea. We could so something like that" or "Next time I think we should . . . ." It was clear that their thinking had not ended because they had reached the day of the competition.

Partner up with another class to run a competition. Having classes compete against each other in a good-natured way can help limit problems within the class while still offering the benefits of competition. It also creates the added benefit of giving you a colleague to plan with.

This is also a strategy that is easy to start small with. You could begin by planning a period-long game show–style quiz as a starting point. Even this amount of competition can lead the way to something with additional depth, where you might bring other staff or students in to act as judges for the two classes.

Limit the extent to which winning and losing takes place. Avoid making the winners too proud or losers too dejected. One way to do this is to structure the winnings in a more egalitarian way. You might, for example, have a first- and second-place winner and then the rest of the groups as runner-ups. This still allows the excellence in the groups to be noted while eliminating having an actual last-place group, which can be dispiriting.

Have students evaluate their own performances. It's important to have students reflect on what went well and what they can improve on for next time, regardless of whether they won or lost. Being focused on continuous improvement is vital in a world that is continually changing, as is learning to be objective about ourselves and our performance. Ask students to provide evidence in their self-evaluation so that their ideas are rooted in reality and not just their self-perception.

Keep it fun. Use the competition to provide a starting and end point, but keep the focus on the work, not the competition itself. If the competition is becoming more important than the work, it's time to have a classroom conversation or change the structure of the competition. The competition is there to provide some excitement and challenge, but ultimately it is there to serve the learning and not the other way around.

Overcoming Obstacles

Like any strategy, using competition can have its challenges. Here are some of the most common ones and how to deal with them.

Students are taking the competition too seriously. If the competition is overtaking the work, as referenced above, it's time to have a class conversation and rejigger the terms of the contest if necessary. The competition is intended to provide additional motivation, not become the sole source of motivation.

If the work they are doing is important, this is not likely to be as much of a problem. For example, if students are working on a social justice issue that is deeply meaningful to them, then whether they win or lose is not as important because they are taking satisfaction from the work itself. No one left the Venture Education competitions feeling dejected because they had done great work that they were proud of, and seeing the great work of others made them want to be better themselves, which is of course the ultimate goal.

Some students are poor losers or bad winners. One of the reasons we need to embrace competition is so we can have discussions about how to win and lose graciously. Talk ahead of time with students about what good winning and good losing looks like so that they are clear on each. It would also be wise to remind students of these characteristics before announcing who won.

Take Students into the Community

Learning doesn't need to take place in a classroom. One of the easiest ways to start students thinking differently about the world around them is to take them into it. Like with many of the strategies in this book, there are important lessons to be learned by going into the community that are not explicitly stated in most curricula. Communicating respectfully, exploring potential partnerships, and considering how we conduct ourselves in the presence of strangers are all vital skills.

Where Do I Begin?

There are a number of ways to bring students to the community or bring the community to them.

Plan a trip before the end of the year. Too often, trips out of the school are done at the end of the school year as a reward for the work that students have done. While this is a fine way to connect with students, it can send the message that the important learning is already done, so we can go and do something fun. Learning can and should be fun at any time of the year. Getting into the community is too important to be left until the month of June. Trips often help us to get to know our students better and bond with them in ways that we couldn't during a regular class. By planning trips earlier, we can benefit from our increased knowledge about our students while we still have them.

In the South Branch project, we purposely took all the students away to a leadership camp at the beginning of the school year because we wanted to get to know them better and create group cohesion through the shared experience. They engaged in many problem-solving activities and trust games, which also reinforced this goal. Class trips, where resources allow, are a powerful teaching strategy and not just something fun to do.

Think locally. Planning a trip doesn't mean it has to be a multiday, overseas adventure. Many schools have resources within walking distance that could enhance learning. Remember to think creatively. Just because you don't have a museum next door doesn't meant there aren't educational places to go. For example, a retirement home across from our school has been the source of many educational opportunities: placements for cooperative education, a place to volunteer, a source of an appreciative audience for a music or drama program, and a place to interview residents with a lifetime of experience and memories. Student visits to the home are as beneficial to the residents as they are to the students. Parks, government offices, private businesses, historical sites, and other public spaces can all be used as jumping-off points for lessons about a wide range of subjects. Even a walk around the neighborhood can start discussions around geography, history, architecture, politics, ecology, sociology, art, and economics, to name a few.

Bring the community to you. Sometimes it's easier, more practical, and safer to have the community come to you. Guest speakers or facilitators can be an important addition to the classroom experience. As discussed earlier in the chapter, ensuring that you've had a fulsome discussion with your guest to discuss expectations, how best to work with your class, timing, and what you are both hoping to get out of the experience will increase the chances of success.

Remember that the most successful partnerships are ones where the partner is supporting the work the students are doing rather than simply talking to them about something for an hour. In the South Branch project, having the head of planning coming to talk to the students for an hour about urban planning would have been a lot different than the ongoing partnership we had to design a new park. Whether you're planning a field trip or guest speaker, always try to make a deeper connection to the work the students are doing.

Overcoming Obstacles

Sometimes, things don't go as well as we'd like when taking students into the community. Here are some tips to increase the likelihood of success.

Student behavior was poor outside the school. Ensure that you've had adequate discussion with the students ahead of time and addressed the following issues:

- Give specific examples so that students have a clear understanding of what desirable behavior looks like. Focusing on the behaviors you want to see, rather than those you don't, builds students up instead of criticizing them.
- Encourage students to speak politely and help them frame positive ways to start conversations and ask questions respectfully.
- Provide students with some specific goals that you have for the visit, and ask them what their goals are so that you are both clear on what success looks like.
- Talk to students about what it means to be representatives of the whole school when they are in the community and how their actions can affect community perception of the entire building. Self-respect is something we want students to consider in their behavior.

Taking It to the Next Level

Connecting student work to the community is a good starting point for making it relevant. Thanks to technology, it's become easier than ever to access different types of communities all over the world.

Engage students with online communities. Technical issues have decreased dramatically over the last decade, and most people now have the technology required to videoconference right from their phones.

While many students use social media in various forms, the fact is that most of what they do tends to be purely social. Powerful tools are used to share funny videos rather than seen as a source of deep learning. You can make good use of these tools. For example, Skype in the Classroom provides a community structure where teachers from around the world can look for other classes to pair up with of similar age and in subject areas of interest.

Reach out to subject area experts, or partner with another class in another part of the world. There are countless opportunities to connect with experts in museums, universities, and other not-for-profits. For example, when students at Linklater Public School were studying ancient history, the school's librarian connected the students to a museum curator in Greece who walked around the museum, showing them antiquities and answering questions via Skype in the Classroom. The technology is available for most devices these days and often underused in educational settings. While an actual trip to Greece would have been incredibly expensive and required substantial planning, the online world is able to transport students there, give them a tour of a museum, and bring antiquities to life, all from the comfort of their own classroom.

Create an online community. Some teachers are using class or individual Twitter accounts to allow students to interact with each other, family members, and outside experts. Showing students the power of social networks can open up an entire world of resources and ideas that they never considered before. As with any online activity, it's important to discuss safety and appropriate behavior.

Publish their work online. There are countless free options for students to create wikis, blogs, or otherwise post their work online. A good starting point may be to find out which social media platforms they are using most regularly and go to where they are. This will help to make them more aware of their own activities online, while also understanding the potential power of the medium.

Go on virtual tours, or have students create their own virtual tour. Many museums, historical sites, and other not-for-profits have created virtual tours on their websites. Platforms like Google Earth can allow students to create their own virtual tours. Students can engage in a rich dialogue about what they would want other people to see in their surrounding communities. They will probably learn a lot about their own neighborhood while creating a tour.

Reflection

Ask yourself the following questions to help to ensure that student work in your class is important enough to share outside the school:

- Do students believe the work that they are doing currently is important?
- Is there currently a wider audience for their work than their teacher?
- Could they name people outside of their parents/guardians and teachers who would be interested in what they are doing?

- Is their work acting as a natural springboard to new forms of collaboration or projects inside and outside school?
- Are they motivated to do their best?
- Do students work collaboratively as a cohesive team to accomplish important goals?
- Would the students feel proud to share the work they are doing currently? Would you?
- Do students feel connected to their broader community through the learning they are doing?
- Are students compelled to do their best because they feel like the work they are doing is important?

Final Thoughts

What can students come up with when you create space for their learning, give them a meaningful challenge, and then reinforce for them the importance of their work? Here's a summary of some of the projects from the last round of Venture Education competitions:

- Grades 4–6 students from S. J. McLeod PS wanted to bring farmers and the local conservation authority together for a one-day symposium to discuss sustainable farming practices and how the community could best work together to maintain good water quality for farmer, residents, and wildlife alike.

- Students from Vanier PS wanted to "build bridges through birthday boxes." In looking for community partnerships, they found a local charity that supported children in an orphanage near Chernobyl. Heartbroken to hear that the children wouldn't normally get birthday parties, they endeavored to raise funds and mail materials to allow them to have the party the students from Vanier thought they deserved.

- Grades 7–8 students from Almonte District High School worried about the risk of concussions to members of the school's football teams. They wanted to raise funds to buy equipment that would go on athletes' helmets and allow them to track potential head injuries.

- Intermediate students from Seaway District High School learned about debilitating infections caused by sand-flea bites in the Third World and began a drive to collect and ship gently used footwear to prevent this.

- International high school students who attended Gananoque Secondary School pitched the idea of connecting young Chinese students with Canadian senior citizens via Skype. They would charge the Chinese students a small amount to partner them up to practice their English with a native speaker, while also combating loneliness and boredom in a local seniors' residence.

As you can see, there are a number of things that are notable about the list:

- There is a huge range in the ideas that students dreamed up, and yet all of them have value. The open-ended challenge allowed students to find themselves in it whether their interest was in technology, social issues, the environment, overseas development, or even agriculture. Students created their own relevance in the space provided.

- Students made a terrific effort in what they were doing, and many of them made good progress with their projects even in the 8 to 10 weeks they had to prepare. Students were excited enough about what they were doing to work on their project during the evenings and on weekends. One of the students described the process as "life-changing."

- Some of the ideas are more practical than others and may have a higher likelihood of success, but all of the ideas are worthy of additional exploration. In many cases, the students had already taken several steps toward doing so.

- This is not a list that would be reasonable to expect a teacher to come up with. The ideas required a team of students collaborating in areas that they were passionate about.

- None of these ideas would have gotten out of the concept stage without the sage guidance, gentle nudging, and resource acquisition of teacher partners. The teachers clearly had a vital role to play, although different from the one they might have played in a traditional classroom.

We all want to find meaning in our lives, students and teachers alike. We derive personal satisfaction from work that is important, which in turn will drive us to be our best. We want our students to be driven by important work. In fact, we want them to thrive on it. Students who actively seek out work that has meaning are going to have an impact on the world and satisfaction in their lives. It's hard to imagine a more important goal for education.

But what about the risks inherent in this kind of education? The fact that students are headed into uncharted territory increases the chances for potential problems, but it's also one of the reasons this type of education is so vital to students' future success. It's not until the teacher steps to the side that student learning reaches its deepest levels. In this move, we find deeper satisfaction while simultaneously increasing the width and depth of student learning, a concept we'll explore in more detail in the next chapter.

Follow the (Student) Leaders

Step 5: Follow the (Student) Leaders

The Big Ideas

- Remember that students are constantly learning.
- Default to yes.
- Avoid riding to the rescue.
- Involve students in curricular decisions.
- Embrace your changing role.

Activation Questions

How much of the instructional time in your class is directed by students' initiative?

When giving students a task, how much time will you leave them to struggle with a problem before you intervene?

To what extent are your students aware of the curriculum and involved in discussions about how best to show their learning?

For the past several years, students in our district have been asked to complete a survey to provide feedback about their involvement, interest level, homework habits, and sense of belonging at school. The survey provides interesting information, but the staff struggle with what to do with the results.

Inspired by my colleague from a neighboring high school, principal Ron Ferguson, we challenged a few members of the student council to find someone completely different from them and to review the survey results. The resulting group of 15 students, from a range of grades, included academically oriented students, athletes, artists, and those only mildly engaged in school.

Over the course of several meetings, the students focused on the keywords *relevance, technology, trust, truancy,* and *school spirit.* I charged them to come up with a plan that would address these issues. Their feedback looked something like this:

- Students feel school isn't relevant because it's not connected to the world around it. This lowers student engagement and school spirit.

- Many students have no idea what they want to do when they finish school. They need to be exposed to more professions, activities, and ideas from the community.

- Students who skip class regularly would be less likely to do so if they felt really connected to the school for at least part of the day.

- The school should offer a series of practical extracurricular courses on a wide range of topics—from gardening to computer game development to baking to charity event planning. This way, students could try out a variety of activities that might help them discover areas of interest to pursue.

- The project should be called Bear University (the bear being the school mascot) to help promote the idea of postsecondary education to all students and encourage those who aren't currently thinking about attending a college or university.

- All students and staff should be allowed to sign up for courses. Courses could be run by staff, students, or outside experts. If a teacher wants to take the course, he or she could act as both supervisor and participant. Having students and teachers learning together would promote a love of learning throughout the school.

- The school should offer practical one-off courses—on how to do taxes, save for school, or get car insurance—under the title of Life 101 because students want to know how to do these things.

- On course completion, participants should receive certificates (to help with résumé building) and public recognition (to promote school spirit and inclusion). It's difficult for students to write a résumé when they have no experience, so including the certificates would help.

- Teachers could connect work done in Bear University to their own course content. The two learning opportunities playing off each other would create more engagement and relevance schoolwide.

Students were invited to share the plan with staff members, who were deeply impressed with its thoughtfulness and flexibility. They also acknowledged that the plan addressed all the students' concerns, which was no small feat (Hardie, 2015).

Remember That Students Are Constantly Learning

The notion that students aren't learning is a fallacy. The bigger issue is that they aren't always learning what we want them to learn in the context that we want them to learn it.

I recall a conversation many years ago with a couple of boys in a small rural school where I was teaching special education. It was winter, and the boys were avid snowmobilers. As we sat down to work on some math, I asked them about their weekend. Both boys, who had learning challenges, spoke excitedly about engines they had rebuilt on the weekend and all the things they had tried before tracking the problem, as well as the pride of hearing the motor come to life. I'd provide more detail about the conversation, but to this day I don't know nearly as much about engines as they did and still can't explain what they did. I was struck at that time by how much learning they had done, how confident they were in the learning, and how relevant it all seemed to them that at the end of the process there was a snow machine waiting to ride across the countryside. Their difficulty with the abstraction of the math shouldn't have been a surprise. Their learning was far more practical, in the immediate term, than anything that was going on at school that, for the most part, they didn't really like. I did my best to bring math into context by bringing in catalogs of engine parts, as many teachers would, but the fundamental gap between how they learned and the abstraction of traditional schooling was not easily bridged. If the math had been more directly applicable to engine repair, and if the knowledge allowed them to *do* something they couldn't have done otherwise, they would have been far more engaged.

A more recent example involved talking with a couple of the occasionally more challenging students at the school about a game they were playing on their phones. They were hooked on an app called Plague Inc. I asked them about the game, and they explained that the goal was to try to destroy all life on earth by releasing pathogens, clearly a provocative prospect for teenage boys. They described in some detail the pros and cons of various pathogens, the effects of various ways to combat their infections, and how different types of disease spread. A discussion with a biology teacher afterward confirmed that much of what they were talking about was scientifically accurate and led to a broader discussion about both gamification and the use of the app in biology class in the future as a way to both teach and engage.

Herein lies an important consideration: Building engagement in school is not about throwing out the curriculum and having students spend all their time in small engine repair (though some of this would no doubt be both beneficial and practical). It's about shifting the context of learning so that it becomes immediately relevant to students.

Where Do I Begin?

Bringing more student leadership and ownership to the classroom starts with the students themselves tapping into their interests and passions.

Bring the learning students are already doing into the classroom. It's important to help students bridge the divide between home learning and school learning, which are fundamentally the same thing at their core. Creating regular opportunities to allow students to present things they are learning outside school will help validate their learning and teach you a lot about them, which can then in turn be used to drive learning ideas.

Have conversations with students about how they learn best. It's important for students to be metacognitive about their learning because it will help them in future learning. It's particularly important for struggling learners to have the learning that they are doing validated and for them to understand that different does not mean worse, which is the unfortunate subtext that school communicates to many of them.

For example, there are countless self-evaluation tools that measure multiple intelligences that can be used with the entire class. These tools can be helpful, especially at the beginning of the year, to both teach us about our students and allow the students to see each other as having a range of talents. This levels the playing field for those who may have strengths that don't always line up with the strengths that we traditionally value in schools. If we have a room full of students who learn best when they are up and moving, there's no sense in trying to make them sit quietly. We need to meet students where they are.

Overcoming Obstacles

Years of schooling can make this change a challenge. Here are some additional thoughts about managing potential difficulties.

Students don't want to learn anything. Students who have reached this level of passivity have likely experienced a long line of frustrations, feelings of incompetence, and negative interactions throughout their school career. They may also not see themselves reflected in the school. The key to motivating students who have reached this state is to take the learning to them. What do they do outside school? What do they want to learn about? Use their interests outside school as a jumping-off point to in-class learning. Finding ways to tap into their passions is the first step toward reengagement.

That's not to say that this is always easy. It can be difficult to undo years of frustration for a student, but in my experience, these are often the students most excited about doing school differently and the source of your greatest pleasant surprises.

Default to Yes

Seventh graders at Carrie P. Meek Elementary School were challenged by their teacher, Isaiah Thomas, to participate in Project Citizen. The purpose of the project is to engage students in learning about public policy by picking an issue that is important to them, researching it, and developing an action plan to help address it.

Thomas started by asking students to bring in headlines of issues in the local community. After headline after headline referred to gun violence, the students declared that this is what they wanted to focus on. Having grown up in the area, Thomas was initially hesitant because he's "had classmates, friends, die from guns. So it's a touchy topic and it's personal to me, but through the class discussion, I saw how personal it was to them. I was like, 'This is the topic.' Because if the students understand and they feel something, they'll work to achieve and work to accomplish this" (Veiga, 2016). Tragically, one of the students lost her little brother to gun violence weeks into the project, reinforcing the deeply personal nature of the issue.

After researching other jurisdictions, interviewing community leaders, and surveying other students, the class developed ideas around how to create improved witness protection laws, better after-school programs for students, and a social media campaign, and they discussed the need to offer conflict resolution to all students.

> Thomas noted that through the project he had seen a shift in student attitude from a
> sense of hopelessness and loss to a sense of empowerment (Veiga, 2016).

Connecting the work to the students and their experiences is a necessary first step. Learning has to be connected to something we already know. By shifting focus toward the students' lives, we can also change the classroom environment.

One way we can start to change the tone of our classrooms is by trying to default to yes whenever possible, even when it might be difficult. Our no's tend to be reflexive and ingrained. They are based on tradition and expectation. For example, when the class asks to continue to work on something when our lesson plan says we are moving on to something else to cover the curriculum, we often insist on moving on. Interrupting engaged learners in the classroom doesn't make much sense, and it's important to challenge our own thinking about when we say no and why.

Where Do I Begin?

Moving the default to yes means that we are validating students and their role in the classroom, as well as their personal experiences. Here are some tips to get started.

Track how frequently you say yes and no. Remember that every time you say no to the students, it detracts from their sense of ownership in the classroom. Track for a day or two how frequently you respond to students with a positive rather than a negative. What messages are you sending, both implicitly and explicitly, to the class? Is the classroom *your* classroom, or is it a negotiated space where you come together to learn?

Take a moment to think before saying no. Are you saying no for a good reason, or is your response purely reactive and based on past practice? Thinking through your own justification for your response will help you to challenge your own preconceived notions about what can and can't be done in the classroom.

Strive for ways to get to yes. Sometimes we simply can't say yes because of practical or safety reasons. We can, however, look at ways we can potentially compromise so that we can meet students in the middle. Meeting students in the middle validates their ideas, while still allowing us to meet professional obligations. It also helps us model how to work in a group.

Overcoming Obstacles

Moving toward saying yes to students can have its challenges. Students will naturally push up against boundaries to see what they can get away with. Here are some potential concerns and responses.

Students are trying to take advantage of my newfound flexibility. Defaulting to yes does not mean giving in to unreasonable or unsafe demands. There will be times where no is the only reasonable response, and that's OK.

One way to turn the discussion around may be to provide students with criteria for a proposal to be accepted. For example, you might tell them, "We can do something different, but it has to be safe, you need to demonstrate to me through the work that you understand this curriculum expectation, and you need to create a product I can evaluate." This creates room for negotiation while redirecting students away from unacceptable ideas.

Avoid Riding to the Rescue

The single biggest mistake most teachers make in the classroom on a regular basis is being too helpful. This sounds a little counterintuitive, but it's a major problem. Jumping in to help too early has the following negative repercussions:

- It inadvertently sends the message to students that they can't do something.
- It doesn't allow students enough think time to work through an issue they may well be able to solve.
- It causes students to see you as the fount of all knowledge rather than as a fellow learner.
- It tells students that they don't have to struggle to understand a concept because you will just give them the answer in the end.
- It lets students know that speed is more important than depth.

Where Do I Begin?

It turns out that being too helpful is not helpful at all. Here are some ways we can avoid these negative outcomes.

Provide adequate think time. Students are frequently impatient and have been trained by years of traditional schooling that the teacher will do the work for them and give the answer if they ask for help. This is not preparing them for the future.

Build in adequate think time to work. Research on the subject says that the average teacher waits between 0.7 and 1.4 seconds before expecting a response to a question. The fact is, many of us don't provide nearly enough time for students to come up with an answer. The research goes on to say that *waiting even three seconds* will increase the quality, length, and number of responses and reduce the number of times a student will say, "I don't know" (Stahl, 1994).

If students are stuck, give them only the most minimal assistance they need to get started. Sometimes students are at a complete impasse and need a hand to get started. Too often, we give them steps 1 through 4, when all they needed was step 1 to get unstuck.

Oftentimes, the best approach is asking a well-worded question rather than providing an answer. Questions that get students to reflect on false assumptions they are making ("How do you know that's the case?"), to consider other approaches ("What are some other possible approaches you could take to this?"), or to come back to the main goals of the project ("Taking a step back, what is it you are working to accomplish here?") can all gently nudge students in the right direction while not denying them the chance to solve the problem or issue.

Have students use other students as a resource. One effective strategy that teachers use is to refuse to answer a student's question unless they've asked at least two other students first. This can take a little practice, but usually after a week of prompting, students will ask classmates first. This strategy helps build cohesion in the class and prevents the teacher from having to answer every single question asked in the room, which is not a good use of human resources.

Overcoming Obstacles

For many students, having the teacher provide the answer is a time-tested strategy. They may not be in a rush to give this shortcut up; here are some thoughts about how to manage this.

Students are getting frustrated because the teacher won't help them. It's entirely natural that this will be the case at the beginning. By using the ask-two-other-students-first strategy above, students will avoid coming to you first, but it also doesn't require them to ask everyone in the class before they can come and speak to the teacher. Engaging students in work that doesn't have right or wrong answers will also help.

Sharing the reasons for why you have changed the way you look at helping them is an important part of the process. Students are more flexible than we give them credit for, and when we provide a reasonable rationale for change, they are usually amenable to it.

Involve Students in Curricular Decisions

As discussed back in Step 2, Contextualize the Curriculum, students often have a surprisingly limited relationship with the curriculum. One of the most challenging aspects of teaching is feeling that you need to constantly dream up amazing, engaging lesson plans and that you have the monopoly on and responsibility for everything creative that is going to take place in the class. This is both daunting and unfair to you. One of the ways we can enhance leadership in the classroom is by involving students in curricular decisions.

Where Do I Begin?

There are a number of entry points to start to build a relationship between your students and the curriculum.

Ask students for their input into how they can demonstrate the skills and knowledge in the curriculum. Every classroom is full of people with creative potential. Start small by sharing one or two curricular expectations with students, and ask them what they need to learn and how they could demonstrate it to you. Engaging students in this work will help them see that while the *what* of what they need to learn is clear, *how* they demonstrate their learning is often quite flexible.

For example, very few, if any, curricula state explicitly that the expectations from the curriculum need to be demonstrated in the form of a written test, yet this is probably the most frequently used product. Having students brainstorm how they can demonstrate their learning will dramatically increase your pool of available ideas, while simultaneously increasing student engagement because they will have ownership of the co-constructed work.

Construct learning goals and success criteria with your students. Once the students have contributed ideas about how the learning will take place in the classroom, it also makes good sense for them to have input into how the work that they will be doing will be evaluated. A classroom discussion about what good work looks like is a necessary precursor to seeing students produce good work.

By defining overall learning goals and creating success criteria with the students, we can dramatically increase the chances of getting the work that we were hoping to get at the end. Students increase their understanding as well as their buy-in to the process. This approach also tends to be successful because learning goals and success criteria are written in language that students clearly understand; this is not always the case with a teacher-created rubric. We'll discuss this idea in more detail in the next chapter.

Overcoming Obstacles

The unique structure and language of a curriculum document can be a challenge for students who have never seen it before. Here are some ways to help them connect.

Students don't understand the curriculum. As mentioned earlier, it will be necessary to interpret the language for younger students. You might show them the original text but then create a learning goal with them in language they understand, which helps them to get the spirit of the text while also being clear on what is expected of them.

The students don't seem very interested in the curriculum. The curriculum itself may not be a great source of inspiration to the students. Many curricula are written in dry, pedantic language. What students are more likely to get excited about is the idea that they can contribute to how the class itself is structured, what kinds of work they are doing, and how the work is being evaluated.

Returning to the earlier discussion about making meaning from the curriculum, this is also an opportunity to talk with students about why these particular skills or pieces of knowledge were deemed important enough to make it into the curriculum. More importantly, it allows us to discuss what you *do* with them, which is the real trick to making work meaningful.

It's also the case that working with the students on the curriculum frames the curriculum as a challenge for both you and them; you are now a team working through it together, rather than a single teacher delivering the curriculum to the students. The students may not necessarily enjoy reading the curriculum, but they will be engaged by the possibilities they can come up with when using it as a jumping-off point.

Embrace Your Changing Role

Giving students an increasing amount of leadership in the classroom can seem disquieting at first. It's not what school is *supposed* to look like. The good news is that it's better for student and teachers, too. Turning some of these roles over to the students gives us more time to do things we want to do: provide students really useful feedback, get to know students as learners and people, enjoy the quality of the work being done in the class, and work *with* our students, rather than *for* them.

Where Do I Begin?

Here are some thoughts about how to begin to make this shift.

Start small. It's not necessary to toss out everything you've done up to this point in your career. Choose one or two of the strategies listed to start making changes. Work through a single curricular expectation with students to see how it goes and work out the bugs. Explain to students why you are trying something different so they get a sense of the broader philosophy behind it. When they understand that this is, fundamentally, about giving them more say in their education and improving their learning, they will be more cooperative than if the changes seem haphazard.

Conference with your students. Having students take on greater roles in the classroom frees you up to meet with individual students, review their work with them, and explain their strengths and next steps. Conferencing is a great strategy that isn't always easy to do in a traditional classroom. Students really value having individual time with their teachers, even if it's just for five minutes, so that they have a clearer sense of what you appreciate in their work and what you need to see from them to improve. It's not practical to conference with all students every day, but it is a good idea to set aside time every day while groups are at work to connect with individual students about their learning. We'll discuss this in more detail in the next chapter.

Encourage your colleagues to experiment with student leadership, too. By sharing some of our early successes and the benefits of having students play a larger part in the classroom, we can start to create a professional discussion with colleagues about these new approaches. Having other adults to bounce ideas around, share tips, and problem solve with can be very valuable for our own professional learning.

Share this information with students, too. Let them know that adults continue to work in collaborative groups to improve learning, too: "Remember that problem we ran into yesterday? Well, I was collaborating with Ms. Smith yesterday, and she had a great solution for us."

Overcoming Obstacles

Teaching in a way that looks different from how we were taught can be uncomfortable because it's so unlike what we are used to. Here is how to address one of the challenges.

Teachers sometimes don't feel like they are teaching anymore. Because much of what is suggested here does not fit with traditional constructs of school, it can feel a little unnatural. In our minds, this isn't what "teaching" looks like.

What's important to remember is that school is not actually about teaching, it's about learning. While the shift in focus sounds subtle, it's not. Learning is an internal process that can be positively influenced by skilled teachers, but it can't be forced. At the end of the day, students have to be actively involved.

I recall from my own practice that it felt odd the first time I walked into a classroom and each of my groups reported to me what their plan was for the period. Once you get over the shock of students planning the learning experience for the day, it's incredibly liberating. Instead of talking for an hour, redirecting students who are losing focus, and answering countless questions, you can circulate and talk to groups, spend time brainstorming problems with them, ask them probing questions to help take their work to the next level, and conference with individual students to help them with their personal learning journey. You are now the elusive guide on the side.

Taking It to the Next Level

Once you have grown confident in student leadership abilities, here are some more advanced ideas about where to take the work.

Involve students in long-range planning. Once you are comfortable with involving student leadership in day-to-day decisions, engaging them in longer-term planning is the next logical step. Inviting students into the process will help them understand how time is a resource and that it's a finite one at that. This strategy can also be paired with connecting students with the curriculum. For example, you might challenge students to plan a week of learning that will involve exploring a certain number of curricular expectations.

Have the students try teaching. Students will learn a deeper appreciation for teaching's challenges while also taking pride in leading the class through learning. Students who are going to teach a concept need to know and understand it thoroughly if they are going to respond to questions and clarify confusion for classmates. Putting students into the role of teacher gives them an increased understanding about learning.

Reflection

Here are some questions to get you started on further developing the role of students as leaders in your classroom:

- How much of what is currently being done in your class is determined by your students?
- To what extent are you working harder than the students in your class, both during class and between classes?
- What elements of your current program could be improved by student input?
- To what extent is the amount of time you are spending in front of the class preventing you from being able to have a clear sense of the learning of all the students in your class, as well as making it difficult to provide personalized feedback to them?
- How much time have your students spent with the curriculum (or your simplified interpretation of it)?
- Are you providing adequate think time?
- Do you currently say yes more than you say no to student ideas?

Final Thoughts

Bear University turned into an exciting initiative. The resulting courses that students organized–on topics as diverse as photography, costuming, cake decorating, and law enforcement–were a great success and saw excellent participation because they focused on students' areas of real interest and gave students insights into a variety of possible careers. In many cases, we brought in experts to teach the courses, which lent them an air of legitimacy. For example, two photographers from the Associated Press taught the photography course. Teachers participated as fellow learners, enjoying the opportunity to become students again.

What the project demonstrated most importantly is that leaving students out of genuine leadership at the school level is a missed opportunity. They are uniquely positioned to make judgments about the quality and effectiveness of school because, ultimately, they are the consumers of the system. Like so many issues in school, this is not about the adults working harder; it's about tapping the potential of the students and making them genuine partners in our drive to make school better.

Reenvision Feedback and Evaluation

Step 6: Reenvision Feedback and Evaluation

The Big Ideas

- Start with meaning.
- Co-create assessment criteria and learning goals.
- Provide more feedback and less evaluation.
- Enjoy grading.

Activation Questions

How frequently do you provide students formative feedback as opposed to evaluations of their work?

What evidence do you have that students are clearly learning and improving through the feedback and evaluation you are providing?

How much time do you spend grading at home versus conferencing with students during class time?

When the team of students creating custom cell phones cases, described at the beginning of Chapter 4, got to the end of their course, they did something remarkable. The curriculum we were working with said that teachers could assess student work through conversation, observation, and product. They asked whether they could record their final thoughts in the form of a video, which they did. Here is a little bit of what they said (edited for brevity and clarity):

> "Today we're going to talk about the different (curricular) expectations we reached with this course and the different activities we did to demonstrate these expectations, and how we believe we hit every overall expectation with the things we did."

> "As part of preparing for the process we had to create a venture plan. I took a grade 11 accounting textbook and learned the concepts to help us set up a proper financial plan."

> "Under the curricular expectation around human resources, we also looked at hiring a subcontractor through the online contractor website oDesk and explored the possibility of hiring someone to help speed up our designs."

> "Another problem we ran into were the limits of computers and tech—how much we could push our computers to achieve different designs and actually make what we wanted—and sometimes we just got stuck."

The video is remarkable on multiple fronts: (1) the students had a clear sense of what their strengths and next steps were for each of the curricular expectations, (2) they were able to provide specific examples to back up their self-assessment, and (3) they likely had a clearer sense of what was in the curriculum, and a better sense of how to assess it, than some educators who are new to the profession. Providing a grade and report card comment for these students couldn't have been easier, short of having them input them into the computer themselves. The only question was which superlatives to use when complimenting their outstanding work. Unfortunately, grading is not always this easy or fun.

If you are feeling bored while grading student work, there's a good chance that they might have been feeling similarly disengaged when creating it. One of the reasons I personally become so passionate about the work in this book is because I shared many of these frustrations with grading. When I began to experiment with more interesting, project-based, real-world work, it became clear (1) how much easier it was to provide meaningful feedback, and (2) how much more fun it is to evaluate work when it's interesting, it varies from student to student, and the quality exceeds expectations.

It is deeply satisfying to write to students and their parents on a rubric or report card about what a great job they did, provide the specifics about the meaningful work accomplished, and suggest next steps that are firmly rooted in the students' work and will be genuinely useful to them going forward.

Start with Meaning

Let's take a moment to return to the beginning of the process outlined in this book, with a focus on meaning, as we contemplate the end. One piece that is often left out of discussions about feedback and evaluation is that it can be difficult because the work did not begin purposefully. It doesn't matter how good your evaluation strategies are if students have been disengaged throughout the learning process, don't see how the work relates to them, and are not excited about what they are doing. Under such circumstances, evaluation can result in one of those situations where the teacher ends up working far harder than the students.

Where Do I Begin?

Here are some thoughts about how to begin the shift in feedback and evaluation practices.

Think about feedback and evaluation that would work in the real world. Does your feedback to students help them get better at practical skills? Is it focused on knowledge that they will continue to find useful going forward? If you find your feedback sounding too much like something only a teacher would understand, take a step back and reexamine the purpose of the work. Effective feedback and evaluation should be clear, easy to understand, anchored in examples, and useful. If it wouldn't make sense to someone in a nonschool setting, it may not be as practical as you would like.

Overcoming Obstacles

Sometimes, if we don't start purposefully enough, student work can become disengaged. Here is a challenge to consider.

It seemed like the work started with meaning, but now it's becoming less clear. As discussed earlier, a well-timed pivot in direction is the sign of a teacher who knows where their class is, what's working, and what isn't. If you find yourself and your students unenthusiastic about the work (and the grading), then it may be time to have a conversation with them about how you could do things more effectively.

Co-Create Assessment Criteria and Learning Goals

One of the most common mistakes teachers make in their approach to grading students is failing to adequately ensure that students have a clear sense of what *good* looks like. Here's a test: ask a group of students to draw an ocelot, tell them it has four legs and black markings, and then see what they draw. Unless they are very knowledgeable about animals, chances are you will get all manner of drawings—things that look like monkeys, beasts that resemble antelopes, something that looks like a dog. The problem is that the students really don't know what you are looking for. In the classroom, we sometimes run into this in the form of the sinking feeling we get as we start into a pile of marking and realize that none of the students created what you had in mind. (For the record, an ocelot, if you haven't already looked it up, looks like a small leopard with an orange and white coat and black, leopardlike spots and lines.)

Where Do I Begin?

A handful of simple strategies can greatly reduce the chance of running into the ocelot dilemma. Here is a list of strategies to point you in the right direction (Davies, Herbst, & Reynolds, 2012):

1. Involve students in co-constructing criteria.
2. Engage students in self-assessment.
3. Increase the sources of specific, descriptive feedback.
4. Assist students to set goals.
5. Have students collect evidence of learning in relation to standards.
6. Have students present evidence of learning in relation to standards.

For a more detailed examination of these strategies, consider picking up a copy of Davies, Herbst, and Reynolds's excellent book *Leading the Way to Assessment for Learning: A Practical Guide.* In the meantime, here are some key strategies that marry nicely with the goals of real-world learning in the classroom.

Co-construct learning goals. When you construct learning goals with students, you will all be reading from the same proverbial page. The learning goals' wording could be borrowed from the curriculum or reworded into something that is clearer and more readily understood by students. Clarifying what you collectively agree they are learning right from the get-go dramatically reduces the chance that you will find yourselves miles apart from each other at the end of the process. By putting those learning goals on an anchor chart, using them to provide formative feedback, and including them in any rubric that you use, alignment can be maintained.

Sample learning goal: Students will write a newspaper article, using the appropriate format, while including tips for the public about how to reduce the environmental footprint of their home.

Co-construct success criteria. While the learning goals give you the overall target, the success criteria tell you how to know if you've achieved the goal. To return to our earlier example, if the learning goal is to create an accurate drawing of an ocelot, then the success criteria say that a student will have accomplished this if the drawing features the following: a medium-sized, catlike animal; an orange and white body with leopardlike markings; a long tail; short ears; green eyes.

Sample success criteria: Students will have achieved success on the newspaper article if it meets the following criteria:

- The article includes a byline.
- It is written in the third-person impersonal and in the present tense.
- The first paragraph of the article answers the 5 Ws.
- People are quoted in the article.
- The article makes clear why people would want to shrink their environmental footprint.
- The news report includes at least three practical tips that most homeowners could use.

You can see from this example why a clear learning goal needs to be further fleshed out with the use of detailed, easy-to-understand success criteria because (1) the criteria are what students will use to determine their own success, (2) they can be used to provide effective peer feedback (peers can use the list to identify missing or incorrect elements), (3) they can be used by the teacher to provide formative feedback, and (4) these criteria can be used to objectively evaluate the article and provide strengths and next steps at the end of the process.

When we assign work to students without taking the time to create criteria with them, we shouldn't be surprised when their picture of an ocelot looks like a lemur.

Refer to the learning goals and success criteria regularly. One mistake that teachers sometimes make, especially when new to these strategies, is to use them at the beginning of the learning process and then forget about them as the work advances. Ensuring alignment between the learning goals and success criteria, regularly referring to them, and using them as a tool to build understanding are all crucial to seeing good products at the end of the process. Consistency and clarity are the keys to success.

Use the learning goals and success criteria for peer and self-assessment. Two strategies that can quickly run into trouble are peer and self-assessment. In the first case, students aren't really sure what they are looking for and will sometimes provide feedback to their classmates that is supportive but not very helpful: "I liked it. I thought it was nice." However, if they have a clear sense of what the target is, they can start to comment on strengths and potential next steps for the work. To return to the goal and criteria above, a peer might say, "Two things that are effective about your news article are that it has a good byline and the first paragraph answers the 5 Ws. As a next step, you may want to edit the last two paragraphs because they slip out of the third person impersonal and use the past tense." Note that the feedback is now both useful and easy to come up with for students who have access to an anchor chart or peer assessment rubric.

Self-assessment often runs into similar hurdles as peer assessment. When asked what they can improve about their work, students will often respond with "I don't know. Make it better?" Again, this really does not help them improve their work. Self-assessment is a skill they need to learn: Being realistic about their work and being able to see how to improve it are skills that will serve them throughout adulthood. If students have a very specific list of criteria to assess their work against, they are far more likely to notice that they are missing something. For written work, another strategy is to give the most important criteria colors and provide students with corresponding highlighters. Ask students to highlight examples of each of the criteria; it becomes far more evident that something is missing when they realize they have nothing to underline for a specific color. For performance-based work, encourage students to record audio or video of their work and use the criteria to assess their performance. By using a recording, they get distance from the work and can focus on their effect on the audience.

Note how the use of the learning goals and success criteria ensures that the feedback is focused on the work and not on the learner. This is crucial because it avoids any potential perception that the criticism is personal. The feedback simply recognizes how far along the learning process the work currently is and gives specific suggestions about how to move it further along this continuum.

Overcoming Obstacles

Co-creating learning goals and success criteria can sometimes lead to problems.

The goals or criteria no longer seem aligned with the work. It's not uncommon for our understanding of what *good* looks like to change as we get further into the work and realize that we've left out important elements or have included some irrelevant elements. Don't be afraid to revisit and revise as necessary.

The students are continuing to produce poor quality peer or self-assessment. Like any skill, providing effective peer and self-assessment requires a certain amount of practice. Anchor the work in the learning goals and success criteria you've co-constructed with students; marry it with a helpful template, rubric, or anchor chart; and model the process for how to use the criteria in classwide discussion.

Provide More Feedback and Less Evaluation

Engaging students in meaningful work makes assessing them much easier. It's also the case that it frees teachers up to circulate the room, connect with individual students, and give them relevant, timely, and personal feedback, which is simply not possible if we spend most of the class talking from the front. Spending time discussing with students what they are doing and providing ongoing feedback means that we need to spend far less time at home making comments on stacks of paper that they only briefly read over and seldom incorporate into their next piece of work.

Where Do I Begin?

Here are some strategies that you can use to start to shift the balance.

Reduce grading wherever possible to stop the myth that learning has an end point. Many students are conditioned to interpret a grade as the completion of the learning process. We want to get students out of the habit of regularly asking, "Is this for a grade?" By focusing on improving work, rather than evaluating it, we can start to shift their thinking.

Make conferences with students a classroom norm and expectation. By selecting even five or six students a day to meet with, we can get through a class in a week or so. Being freed up from grading should allow for this to be built into your schedule. Having students engaged in meaningful work makes conferencing far easier because they are busy working, thus reducing the risks and opportunities for classroom management issues. Regular conferencing will give students valuable personalized feedback to help them develop their work and deepen their learning, as well as opportunities to hone critical life skills such as time management and ownership of their work.

Overcoming Obstacles

One issue that teachers sometimes run into is working harder on the evaluation and the comments than the students did on the assignment. It's also the case that students don't apply the directions from the comment in their next piece of work.

The students are not reading the comments the teacher spent hours writing. Garfield Gini-Newmann, from the Critical Thinking Consortium, makes a very simple and thoughtful suggestion: Provide comments first, grades later. If you make a whole lot of comments on a student's work but also give it a grade, students infrequently read the comments in detail and even less frequently apply them to their next piece of work. Instead, if you provide the comments without the grade, return the work to them, and then give them a few days to make changes and resubmit the work, you don't have to grade the whole thing again. You just have to go over the changes and then assign a grade. You haven't, in fact, done any more work. You've simply moved the valuable comments into the feedback portion of the learning process, which allows students to make corrections and get better.

Enjoy Grading

Let's reflect for a moment on how report card comments for students engaged in some of the projects described in this book could start and how different they could be from traditional report card fare:

- "While presenting to the mayor and town council their ideas for a new municipal park development . . ."
- "In publishing a series of newspaper articles for the local paper designed to shrink the community's environmental footprint . . ."
- "While attending a UN climate change conference . . ."

- "Through the process of repairing bikes for underprivileged students..."
- "In collaborating with an England-based entrepreneur about designs for their latest product..."

What quickly becomes apparent is that (1) the meaningfulness of the work dramatically changes the final evaluation, and (2) these comment starters are exciting and vastly different from typical comments that students and parents receive. The work makes sense to everyone involved in the process—students, teachers, and parents—which helps to alleviate some of the most difficult and frustrating parts of the learning process for all parties. Students enjoy purposeful work. Teachers enjoy marking work that is creative and represents a student's best effort. Parents enjoy their children coming home from school excited and proud of the work they've been doing.

Where Do I Begin?

Here are some things to consider as you work to make the process of feedback and evaluation less onerous.

Consider what students will produce as part of the work. Will they enjoy creating the work? Will you enjoy grading it? If the answer is a clear no to both questions, it's probably time to rethink.

By engaging students in creative work that has space for the learner (as discussed in Chapter 4) with multiple possible outcomes, you are dramatically improving the chances that students will produce a range of work that, when combined with clear learning goals and criteria, will meet your expectations while also being interesting to assess.

Think about what you are *really* trying to assess. There are lots of ways for students to show what they know and what they can do. For example, don't ask students to produce long pieces of writing that will take an extended period of time to grade if (1) that's not the best format to assess their learning, and (2) the learning value of the activity is not worthy of that much time and effort. You might instead have students record a short video showing what they know and respond to them in kind, particularly for learning that is not fundamental but needs to be addressed because it's in the curriculum.

Overcoming Obstacles

Here are some challenges that might emerge.

Some grading is still a drag. Okay, so maybe it's not possible to enjoy grading *all* the time. Some pieces of the curriculum will need to be taught in a traditional way, which in turn is likely to generate traditional grading. Having said that, if you can focus on engaging students in more large-scale projects, which will allow you to spend more time in providing feedback, this will certainly cut down on the amount of grading required.

Having students engage in performance-driven summative evaluations (e.g., making a pitch, giving a formal presentation, speaking to a school assembly, putting on a play, running a workshop for other students, training seniors on how to use social media) rather than written ones can allow you to grade multiple students quickly, while also doing so during the time you are with them. Videotaping performance work, as discussed above, can allow you to revisit the work afterward and can make for a very powerful self-assessment tool for students.

Taking It to the Next Level

Once you have become more confident in providing feedback and evaluation of meaningful work, here is an advanced strategy to consider.

Have students write their own report card comments. Students who have a clear sense of what they are doing well and what they need to work on next—through regular feedback, conferencing, and peer and self-assessment—are often capable of writing their own report card comments. In fact, they should be able to. If students don't know what you're going to write on their report cards at the end of the learning process, then the process itself is likely flawed; finding out what you needed to improve from the report card is of minimal help when it's too late to get better.

One thing to note: often students will be their own worst critics. Using some of what they've written respects their voice, while adding to it to accurately convey your professional judgment will help give them a clearer sense of how they did. This is a strategy that will not be appropriate for some age groups and some individual students. They need to be old enough to manage work of this kind and reflect on their work dispassionately.

Reflection

Here are some questions to consider when reflecting on feedback and evaluation practices:

- Are all the student products exactly the same? If so, could they potentially be altered to allow more student input and creativity?

- How much of your time is spent on feedback versus evaluation? If you are evaluation heavy, how could you alter the structure of your class to ensure that students are getting the feedback they need *during* the learning process and not after it is over?
- Are you spending more time grading than your students spent creating their product or performance? If so, how can you alter the process to ensure that they are the ones most actively involved in their learning?
- Do your students know what they are good at and what they need to work on next?
- Could your students write their own accurate report card comments?
- Is the evaluation process a time of pride in the great strides that students have made and in the quality of their work, or is it a source of frustration? If it's the latter, how could you use some of the strategies in this chapter to tip the balance?
- Can you engage students in deeper learning experiences that will take longer, go deeper, and decrease the amount of time you are spending on evaluation?

Final Thoughts

Feedback and evaluation are vitally important parts of the learning process. In particular, feedback takes us from our current state and helps us to move forward. Too often these processes are sources of frustration for both teachers and students. For teachers, the work is time-consuming and laborious. For students, it is often not clear to them what they did or didn't do to deserve a grade, so they don't alter the quality of their work because they're not sure how to, and then they grow frustrated as they receive the same grade time and time again.

Feedback and evaluation can be improved to be more purposeful and more satisfying to all involved. Feedback can and should be provided daily in the classroom environment and not via mountains of paperwork completed late at night by the teacher. Similarly, high-quality work is quick and enjoyable to assess, and if feedback has been provided throughout the process, then you probably already know what you're going to get before it comes in, making grading a confirmation process rather than a rude awakening.

Some simple changes in practice can increase learning and reduce frustration. It's clearly a win-win for both teachers and students.

Final Reflections

As a former elementary school principal, I used to love stopping by kindergarten, which is like a whole other world. When I entered the room, the students and I would look at each other like we were both some kind of alien species until I sat down in one of those impossibly small kindergarten chairs and began to hear about what they were up to.

One gifted teacher I worked with had a wonderful exploratory structure to her class. Students would move around stations, exploring a wide variety of phenomena in math, science, language, and nature. Students were given time to examine, play, sort, and organize everything from buttons to insects. One of her most laudable practices was her unwillingness to answer questions. While this sounds somewhat antithetical, if students asked her a question about something that she thought, given more time, they might be able to divine themselves, she wouldn't tell them. To an inquiry about the shape of an insect, she would respond to a question with a question—"Why do you think its legs are shaped that way?"—and give me a knowing wink.

How do we get back to this state? How do we get back to the point where schools exist to promote a love of learning? How do we make this true for both the staff and the students in the building?

It's a truth, universally acknowledged, that schools can be better. Attend a national or international conference on education, and one thing that every one has in common is the belief that change is necessary. There's plenty of debate about where to start, what to focus on, and how to do it, but there are very few defenders of highly traditional systems. We all want to be better and know that we can be.

The steps and strategies outlined in this book are intended to help you to start to move toward the kind of system we need, where students are engaged by meaningful work, the curriculum is used as a tool to support learning, there is space for students to find themselves in the classroom, their work is given meaning by stepping beyond the classroom walls, and we follow our students as much as (or more than) we lead them.

School can, and should, be better. A good kindergarten class is evidence that the current state is not a natural one. It's a product of decades of institutionalization. To begin the change, it may be necessary for us to look back with a critical eye on our own educational experiences.

What's interesting is that if you ask an adult about their experience of school, they rarely talk about the learning. They talk about it as an emotional experience: "I loved it/hated it"; "I liked my teacher/hated my teacher"; "It was interesting/boring." If you ask about their favorite experiences, they will often describe ones with a social-emotional component: "I had a great teacher who really cared about us and made learning fun"; "I had a great group of friends that I spent time with"; "I was bullied and often frightened." School in its purest academic form is not particularly memorable; no one says, "We did the best worksheet in grade 5" or "There was a really interesting curriculum expectation in grade 10." The emotional component of learning is oddly absent from the structure and explicit purpose of most schools, though one of the differences between effective and ineffective teachers is that effective teachers understand the importance of the emotional components of teaching. They believe the old truism that students "don't care what you know, unless they know that you care."

Building a better school is as much an emotional process as it is an intellectual one. As educators, we've all had those moments in class—sometimes by design and sometimes by chance—when everything clicks into place and student learning, thinking, and confidence are suddenly on clear display. The experience is visceral. The experiences are also shared: Both teacher and students know it's working. It's like some kind of perfect educational synchronicity. It's something that we *feel*, not something that we think. When it happens, we go home smiling with pride and wonder, "How can I make this happen more regularly?"

One answer is to create circumstances where learning can take off and students can find themselves in the classroom. We rarely experience this educational nirvana when looking over a pile of tests. We may take pride in the work students have done when we grade a good set, but it rarely provokes a shivers-down-the-spine experience. Those tend to come when students are involved in some kind of performance, whether it be sharing their learning from their genius hour project, an art performance on stage, or a sporting event. It's important to note that the steps in this book are designed to promote students' emotional health as much as their intellectual health.

Pursuing these moments of educational perfection are the work of a lifetime. As you experiment with the steps in this book, model risk taking, involve your students in your journey, embrace the satisfaction of your changing role, and when you're not sure what to do, go with what *feels* right.

Appendix

A Real-World Learning Planner

To help you get started, use the following table to structure your real-world learning experiences. Remember to work both backward and forward.

Step 1: Make Meaning Central to Student Work		
The Big Ideas	**Questions for Planning**	**Sample Projects**
Start with meaning.

Provide the opportunity *and* motivation to lead.

Make learning a challenge.

Connect student learning to the real world.

Use backward design to get to where you want to go. | What kind of challenge could you issue to your students to drive their leadership and learning to the next level?

What kinds of opportunities exist in your local community that could form the basis of truly meaningful work?

What issues, ideas, or questions do students have that could be used as a jumping-off point for their learning? | Reduce the environmental footprint of the school and its surrounding community.

Change public perception of your school or community.

Develop a plan to promote interest in and knowledge about historically significant locations in your neighborhood.

Clean up a local waterway or natural environment.

Create an invention that will improve someone else's quality of life.

Start a profitable business.

Develop a social media campaign to bring attention to an issue of importance and lobby for change.

Create an artistic performance or installation that will help the audience see other people in a new light.

Develop and execute a plan that will make the world a better place.

Organize and run a fundraising campaign for a cause you feel passionate about. |

Step 2: Contextualize the Curriculum	
The Big Ideas	**Cross-Curricular Learning**
View the curriculum as a tool.	How many cross-curricular connections can you integrate in your planning? What can you do to make the curriculum a tool-box rather than a checklist?
Make the *why* explicit.	What is your answer to the question "Why are we learning this?" for each of the expectations you've included?
Be flexible.	How can you deepen student learning of all subject areas by limiting the artificial separation of knowledge into subjects?

Sample Products
What products could students create that would make use of the curricular skills and knowledge in a real-world context?   NOTE: When selecting from the list, consider some important questions: What form is most likely to be used in the real world? How will you ensure that students know what *good* looks like? What products make sense given the timeframe and students' developmental stage? What is a reasonable number of options to offer?

Advertisement	Comic strip	Experiment
Advice column	Commercial	Fable or myth
Analogy	Concept map	Facebook wall
Animation	Creative nonfiction	Fake social media account
Artistic interpretation	Dance	Film
Audio recording	Data/analytics visualization	Flow chart
Avatar	Debate	Freestyle (hip-hop)
Blog	Demonstration	Game
Board game	Diary entry	Game show
Book	Diorama	Glossary
Book jacket	Documentary film	Google Earth tour
Brochure	Documented discussion	Graph
Bulletin board	Drawing	Graphic organizer
Cards (playing/task)	E-book	Infomercial
Collage	Environmental study	Instructional video/book
Comedy skit	Essay	Interview

Learning log
Literature circle
Live stream
Magazine
Map
Mobile
Mock court case
Mock-up/wireframe
Model
Monologue
Movie poster
Mural
Museum exhibit
Music performance
News report
Newsletter/newspaper
Panel discussion
Photo album
Pinterest board
Pitch
Podcast
Poem

Portfolio
Post card
Poster
Presentation
Prezi
Puppet show
Rap
Reenactment
Review
Role-play
Rules/framework
Scavenger hunt
Scrapbook
Sculpture
Self-directed short video
Show and tell
Simulation
Skit
Slideshow
Social media campaign
Song
Speech

Start a business
Story map
Survey
Team-building game
Theatrical play
Three-panel display
Time capsule
Timeline
Trip (organize and lead)
Tutorial
Tweets (series)
Venn diagram
Video game
Visualization
Walking tour
Wanted ad
Website
Whiteboard animation
Wiki
Word wall
YouTube channel

Step 3: Create Space to Learn		
The Big Ideas	**Questions for Planning**	**Sample Prompts**
Make room for active learners.	How can you create more space for students by focusing on what they need to while giving them input into how it will be done? What choices can you provide to students to allow them to use their own judgment and to build engagement? How will you find out from students what their learning goals are and how can they track them?	"We're going to work to reduce bullying in the school. How do you think we could do this?" "For this work, you can choose from one of three products, but I want to know why you've chosen the one you did." "We're going to start learning journals to track what your goals are and to gather evidence of how you are progressing."
Create space to fail.	What steps can you take in your practice to start to redefine failure for students not as a negative but as a powerful learning opportunity?	"This year, we're going to approach the fear of failure head-on. What are some of the positive effects of failure? What are some famous failures that lead to amazing things?"
Change the environment to change the learner.	What skills and characteristics do you want your students to develop? How can you alter the classroom environment so that they will adapt accordingly?	"This year, it's important that you all learn to become more independent. Here are some things that I want you to be responsible for . . ."
Resource student work appropriately.	What resources can you provide to students, and give them control over, that will allow them to do their best work and send the message to them that their work is important?	"Each group is going get $20 from the fundraising we did to support your work. How can you ensure that the money goes as far as possible?"
Model lifelong learning.	How do students see your learning as a teacher? Do they know what you're learning and what challenges you've had?	"Every Friday we're going to have four people from the class share what they've been learning outside school. I'm going to put myself into the rotation."

Step 4: Connect Student Work to the Community		
The Big Ideas	**Questions for Planning**	**Sample Prompts**
Form community partnerships.	What organizations, businesses, schools, institutions, and historical, geographical and environmental features are within a few miles of the school? What potential connections are there to big ideas and the curriculum?	"We are going to take a walking tour where we will be looking at historically significant buildings. Three weeks from now, we'll walk the same route again, but each of your groups will provide us with information at each stop, gleaned from research you've done on the building you have selected. We will visit the local museum next week as part of our research."
Give students an audience.	What kind of audiences can you give your students? What is appropriate for their developmental stage? What's a good starting point?	"We are going to invite your parents to come in so you can explain to them how we can save energy as part of our work on climate change. We'll practice by inviting the classroom across the hall to come in first so we can get some feedback."
Recognize the social nature of learning.	How can you establish expectations for effective group work? For the work at hand, how can you ensure that each student had a meaningful role and that you've created balanced groups?	"For our next project, we are going to create a social media campaign about an issue important to you. Roles for group members will include editor, photographer, researcher, writer, and graphic designer."
Embrace competition.	How can you use good-natured competition to encourage deeper learning while also teaching students to be gracious winners and to see losing as a learning opportunity?	"For our next challenge, you will be asked to build a birdhouse for a local endangered species. We will have a biologist and ornithologist come in to act as judges as to which design is the most effective."
Take students into the community.	What are some nearby locations that can engage students and place their learning in the real world? What kind of online community could you connect with to further enrich their learning?	"As part of our work on the war, we will be visiting our local retirement home to speak to residents about their memories of it. We will also connect with a historian at a museum in the United Kingdom via Skype in order to learn more."

Step 5: Follow the (Student) Leaders	
The Big Ideas	**Reflective Practice Questions**
Remember that students are constantly learning.	Can you see evidence of what students are learning outside the classroom and in the discussions and work that are taking place?
Default to yes.	Are you saying yes to students more frequently than you are saying no? When you have to say no, are you looking for ways to suggest acceptable alternatives?
Avoid riding to the rescue.	When you ask a question, are you consciously giving students at least 10 seconds to think about a response?
Involve students in curricular decisions.	Are you inviting students to look at expectations from the curriculum and having discussions with them about how the expectations could be used and what students could do to demonstrate their learning to you?
Embrace your changing role.	As you adjust to your new role, are you taking advantage of the increased autonomy of students to find time to regularly conference with them, provide them feedback, and get to know them better in order to further improve learning?

Step 6: Reenvision Feedback and Evaluation		
The Big Ideas	**Questions for Planning**	**Sample Prompts**
Start with meaning.	How can you ensure a clear connection between purposeful work, the products or performances created, and the evaluation at the end of the process?	"At the end of the project, you will be graded on your demonstration of curriculum expectations through the writing and performance of your one-act play. Your ability to bring the community together through the play will be measured by audience questionnaires."
Co-create assessment criteria and learning goals.	How are you tracking curricular expectations and ensuring that they are being used in a clear and purposeful way? What can you do to ensure that students have a clear understanding of what good looks like and that you all have agreed-upon criteria that will be used to provide consistent, meaningful feedback as well as fair and transparent evaluations?	"Today we're going to learn about rhetorical devices because we can use them to make our grant application more persuasive." "Because each group is going to contribute a chapter to our e-book on the Civil War, it's important that we take some time now to establish what the criteria are for effective writing and a well-constructed chapter."
Provide more feedback and less evaluation.	How can you change the use of time and structure of the classroom to ensure that students get regular, formative feedback and conference with you regularly about important learnings?	"Starting today, I'm going to conference with five of you each period while your group works on the project. This will give me time to give you individualized feedback about how you are doing."
Enjoy grading.	As a result of your changes, are you getting better-quality and creative work from students? If not, why not?	"Thanks to the great work you've been doing, I'm happy to say I'm really enjoying evaluating it and am impressed by your level of success."

References

Azzam, A. M. (2014, September). Motivated to learn: A conversation with Daniel Pink. *Educational Leadership, 72*(1), 12–17. Retrieved from http://www.ascd.org /publications/educational-leadership/sept14/vol72/num01/Motivated-to-Learn @-A-Conversation-with-Daniel-Pink.aspx

Bolak, K., Bialach, D., & Dunphy, M. (2005). Standards-based, thematic units integrate the arts and energize students and teachers. *Middle School Journal, 36*(5), 9–19.

Brenneman, R. (2016, March 22). Gallup poll finds engagement in school dropping by grade level. *Education Week*. Retrieved from https://www.edweek.org/ew/ articles/2016/03/23/gallup-student-poll-finds-engagement-in-school.html

Bringing the community into the classroom. (2016, April 19). *Edutopia*. Retrieved from http://www.edutopia.org/practice/community-partners-making-student-learning-relevant

Costley, K. C. (2015). *Research supporting integrated curriculum: Evidence for using this method of instruction in public school classrooms*. Arkansas Tech University. Retrieved from http://files.eric.ed.gov/fulltext/ED552916.pdf

Davies, A., Herbst, S., & Reynolds, B. P. (2012). *Leading the way to assessment for learning: A practical guide* (2nd ed.). Courtenay, BC: Connections Publishing; and Bloomington, IN: Solution Tree.

Decker, K. (2016, February 16). Growing a community to build a garden. *Edutopia*. Retrieved from http://www.edutopia.org/blog/growing-community-to-build -garden-kathleen-decker

Dewey, J. (1897, January 16). My pedagogic creed. *The School Journal, 54*(3), 77–80.

Dweck, C. (2006). *Mindset: The new psychology of success*. New York: Ballantine Books.

EcoLeague. (2016). EcoLeague success stories: School bike repair program. *Resources for Rethinking*. Retrieved from http://www.resources4rethinking.ca/en/ecoleague/ success-stories

Fleming, J. (2012, September 30). Transcript for Carol Dweck on the psychology of failure and success. *To the Best of Our Knowledge*, Wisconsin Public Radio. Retrieved from http://archive.ttbook.org/book/transcript/transcript-carol-dweck-psychology-failure-and-success

Fletcher, A. (2015). *Meaningful school involvement: Guide to students as partners in school change*. Retrieved from https://soundout.org/wp-content/uploads/2015/06/MSIGuide.pdf

Garner, R. (2015, March 20). Finland schools: Subjects scrapped and replaced with "topics" as country reforms its education system. *Independent*. Retrieved from http://www.independent.co.uk/news/world/europe/finland-schools-subjects-are-out-and-topics-are-in-as-country-reforms-its-education-system-10123911.html

Grimes, S. (2016, March 23). WebSLAM: Real-world problem solving with civic focus. *Edutopia*. Retrieved from http://www.edutopia.org/blog/webslam-problem-solving-civic-focus-shawn-grimes

Hacker, D. J., Dunlosky, J., & Graesser, A. C. (Eds.). (2009). *Handbook of metacognition in education*. New York: Routledge.

Hardie, E. (2015). When students drive improvement. *Educational Leadership, 72*(9), 92–96. Retrieved from http://www.ascd.org/publications/educational-leadership/jun15/vol72/num09/When-Students-Drive-Improvement.aspx

Kapur, M., & Bielaczyc, K. (2012). Designing for productive failure. *Journal of the Learning Sciences, 21*(1), 45–83. doi: 10.1080/10508406.2011.591717

Lamprey, B. & Reilly, B. (2016, July 6). Project Au-Some: Building empathy and collaboration. *Edutopia*. Retrieved from http://www.edutopia.org/blog/project-au-some-building-empathy-collaboration-brenna-lamprey-beth-reilly

Lynette, R. (n.d.). 72 creative ways for students to show what they know. *Minds in Bloom*. Retrieved from https://minds-in-bloom.com/72-creative-ways-for-students-to-show/

McMillan, J., & Tamblyn, R. (2006). Taking a walk on the "real" side. *ETFO Voice*. Retrieved from http://etfovoice.ca/node/24

National Institute of Mental Health. (2015). Anxiety disorders in children and adolescents fact sheet. Bethesda, MD: Author. Retrieved from https://www.naset.org/fileadmin/USER_UPLOADS_PROTECTED/1-New_Content_Files/Files_for_Updated_Links_2013/anxiety-disorders-in-children-and-adolescents.pdf

Ontario Ministry of Education. (2006). The Ontario curriculum grades 1–8: Language [Revised]. Retrieved from http://www.edu.gov.on.ca/eng/curriculum/elementary/language18currb.pdf

Pink, D. (2009). *Drive: The surprising truth about what motivates us*. New York: Riverhead Books.

Riddle, T. (2016, February 17). Empowering students with design thinking. *Edutopia*. Retrieved from http://www.edutopia.org/blog/empowering-students-with-design-thinking-thomas-riddle

Shapiro, D., Dundar, A., Wakhungu, P. K., Yuan, X., Nathan, A., & Hwang, Y. (2015, November). *Completing college: A national view of student attainment rates—Fall 2009 Cohort* (Signature Report No. 10). Herndon, VA: National Student Clearinghouse Research Center.

Stahl, R. J. (1994). Using "think-time" and "wait-time" skillfully in the classroom. *ERIC Digest*. ED370885. Retrieved from http://files.eric.ed.gov/fulltext/ED370885.pdf

Teach Thought Staff. (2018, June 24). 100 things students can create to demonstrate what they know. Retrieved from https://www.teachthought.com/learning/60-things-students-can-create-to-demonstrate-what-they-know/

Veiga, C. (2016, April 15). Miami-Dade student project: Saving themselves, other kids from gun violence. *Miami Herald.* Retrieved from http://www.miamiherald.com/news/local/education/article72003167.html

Wagner, T. (2008). *The global achievement gap.* New York: Basic Books.

Index

About the Author

Eric Hardie is a superintendent of instruction at the Ottawa-Carleton District School Board in Eastern Ontario.

With more than two decades of experience in education, Hardie is a former elementary and secondary school teacher and principal. He holds a degree in English from Western University, a Bachelor of Education from Mount Allison University, and a Master of International Education (School Leadership). He has provided professional development and training in experiential learning, working with both teachers and school leaders, and has previously published articles in ASCD's *Educational Leadership*.

Hardie is committed to writing and developing resources and processes to support the adaptation of innovative teaching practices, connecting schools and the wider world, and focusing on student voice. He has presented in Canada and the United States about entrepreneurship, innovation, and student leadership.

Hardie lives with his wife, three daughters, and black lab, Ellie, in Carleton Place, Ontario. Connect with him via Twitter @eric_hardie.

Related ASCD Resources

At the time of publication, the following resources were available (ASCD stock numbers in parentheses).

Cultivating Curiosity in K–12 Classrooms: How to Promote and Sustain Deep Learning by Wendy L. Ostroff (#116001)

Designed to Learn: Using Design Thinking to Bring Purpose and Passion to the Classroom by Lindsay Portnoy (#120026)

Project Based Teaching: How to Create Rigorous and Engaging Learning Experiences by Suzie Boss with John Larmer (#118047)

Real-World Projects: How do I design relevant and engaging learning experiences? (ASCD Arias) by Suzie Boss (#SF115043)

Setting the Standard for Project Based Learning: A Proven Approach to Rigorous Classroom Instruction by John Larmer, John Mergendoller, and Suzie Boss (#114017)

Students at the Center: Personalized Learning with Habits of Mind by Bena Kallick and Allison Zmuda (#117015)

Teaching in the Fast Lane: How to Create Active Learning Experiences by Suzy Pepper Rollins (#117024)

What If? Building Students' Problem-Solving Skills Through Complex Challenges by Ronald Beghetto (#118009)

For up-to-date information about ASCD resources, go to www.ascd.org. You can search the complete archives of *Educational Leadership* at www.ascd.org/el.

ASCD myTeachSource®
Download resources from a professional learning platform with hundreds of research-based best practices and tools for your classroom at http://myteach-source.ascd.org/

For more information, send an e-mail to member@ascd.org; call 1-800-933-2723 or 703-578-9600; send a fax to 703-575-5400; or write to Information Services, ASCD, 1703 N. Beauregard St., Alexandria, VA 22311-1714 USA.

WHOLE CHILD
TENETS

1 **HEALTHY**
Each student enters school healthy and learns about and practices a healthy lifestyle.

2 **SAFE**
Each student learns in an environment that is physically and emotionally safe for students and adults.

3 **ENGAGED**
Each student is actively engaged in learning and is connected to the school and broader community.

4 **SUPPORTED**
Each student has access to personalized learning and is supported by qualified, caring adults.

5 **CHALLENGED**
Each student is challenged academically and prepared for success in college or further study and for employment and participation in a global environment.

THE **WHOLE** **CHILD**

The ASCD Whole Child approach is an effort to transition from a focus on narrowly defined academic achievement to one that promotes the long-term development and success of all children. Through this approach, ASCD supports educators, families, community members, and policymakers as they move from a vision about educating the whole child to sustainable, collaborative actions.

The Relevant Classroom relates to the **engaged**, **supported**, and **challenged** tenets.

For more about the ASCD Whole Child approach, visit **www.ascd.org/wholechild.**